D1169233

to the Far Right Christian Hater...

You Can Be a

Good Speller or a

Hater,

But You Can't Be Both

to the Far Right Christian Hater...

You Can Be a Good Speller or a Hater, But You Can't Be Both

— Bonnie Weinstein

This is a Genuine Rare Bird Book

A Rare Bird Book | Rare Bird Books
453 South Spring Street, Suite 531
Los Angeles, CA 90013
rarebirdbooks.com

Printed in the United States of America
Distributed in the US by Publishers Group West

10 9 8 7 6 5 4 3 2 1

Publisher's Cataloging-in-Publication data

Weinstein, Bonnie.
    To the far right Christian hater...you can be a good speller or a
hater, but you can't be both / by Bonnie Weinstein.
    p. cm.
    ISBN 978-1-940207-83-4
1. Freedom of religion. 2. Church and state. 3. Religion and law. 4.
Armed Forces—Religious life. 5. Soldiers—Religious life. 6. English
language —Errors of usage. I. Title.

BV741 .W455 2014
323.44/2/0973 —dc23

Dear MRFF,
Just wanted to express my total dismay at your website and purpose in life. So,
please **** YOURSELF!

To the Military Religious Freedom Foundation,
I'll evangelize where ever I like and I don't care what you or the constitution say period. GET IT!!!
-C.I.

If you violate the U.S. Constitution by the time, place, and manner in which you choose to proselytize others with your fundamentalist Christianity, you WILL be punished and held accountable!!!
—Mikey Weinstein, MRFF Founder and President

To the Military Religious Freedom Foundation,
Considering the failure record of the federal government in prosecuting religion, and considering how much even the most tyrannical regimes (i.e. China Roman Empire) have failed in stopping Biblical Christianity your chances of success is nil. There are other who think like me and will take over where I have started and don't finish. So yeah go ahead and try and stop me. Knock yourself out trying. Your prosecution will only strengthen my position not weaken it.
-C.I

INTRODUCTION

My name is Bonnie Weinstein, and I am married to a force of nature.

About forty years ago now, when I was sixteen, my decision to go up to the United States Air Force Academy to meet "real men" set me on a collision course with my future—one that I would never trade away, even though it so often leaves me shaking my head with disbelief and astonishment at the absolute shock of it all.

Kierkegaard has a saying: "Life can only be understood backwards; but it must be lived forwards." While I admit that I tend to understand myself better the more I move forward in life, I have found that I understand nobody better—both forward and backward—than my darling husband. It saddens me, however, to know that, without a doubt, there is no amount of living through this maelstrom of hate and viciousness—all in the name of a benevolent God—that will ever let me come to understand the men and women who write the hideous letters presented here. This book is but a TINY sampling of the thousands we have received, with more coming in on a daily basis. I have chosen to publish this body of gutter-level trash to try and shed some light on the people they affect—myself and those closest to me.

In 2005, my husband and I started the Military Religious Freedom Foundation (MRFF), and in the ensuing decade it has taken an extreme amount of intestinal fortitude to stay the course. We fight against those who, at worst, seem hellbent on dismantling our Constitution, and at best, seem to have little idea of what they are talking about. These authors, and I use that term very loosely, seem to have never made it past a third grade intelligence level both in erudition and education. Simple people skills, which kids learn in kindergarten—such as learning to play well, getting along with people, and understanding that not everyone thinks the same way you do—have sadly eluded them altogether.

Tens of thousands of clients have come to MRFF after being horribly tormented because of their faith or lack of faith. Their angst becomes very understandable when you see the hate in these letters. Our clients have nowhere else to turn. There is no one to stand up for them, to be their voice, to combat the remorseless abuse they face. The Foundation stands for Constitutional issues within a military environment, which is markedly different from the environment of the ordinary citizen of the United States. That enormous distinction is one our detractors do not even remotely comprehend. I now realize all too well that very few people understand the fine and beautiful balance our American forefathers put together in the first sixteen words of the First Amendment: "Congress shall make no law respecting an establishment of religion or prohibiting the free exercise thereof." The writers of angry letters to MRFF seem to have never read the Constitution or its well-established case law, which they profess to grasp so well.

Article VI, Clause 3, in the body of the Constitution, states: "The Senators and Representatives and the Members of several of the State Legislatures, and all executive and judicial Officers, both of the United States, and of the several States, shall be bound by oath or Affirmation, to support this Constitution; but no religious Test shall ever be required as a Qualification to any Office or public Trust under the United States." NO RELIGIOUS TEST SHALL EVER BE REQUIRED AS A QUALIFICATION TO ANY OFFICE OR PUBLIC TRUST! No, they have never read the Constitution.

I never understood, before the beginning of MRFF, how thoroughly infested our military has become with the pushing of the "one and only correct, true religion." They, of course, are the extremists known as fundamentalist or Dominionist Christians. As I have "lived forward," I "understand backward" the extremely serious danger presented by this virulent version of Christianity, pushed by its fanatic adherents. It has become crystal clear to me that when you mess with people's religious beliefs—however misguided and warped they may be—the situation can turn ugly and personal with lightning speed.

It has been well established that when you present a diehard believer with hardened, indisputable facts, facts which clearly dispel their position, it only further reinforces their erroneous belief. Oh, how true that is! The tidal wave of letters that now come into our inboxes everyday at MRFF is literally mind-boggling. Almost all of these letters fall into very specific groups: the "love" letters, the "hate" letters, and the "please explain this" letters. It is the "please explain this" letters that I like to read the most. Don't get me wrong, the letters of support and thanks—the love letters—are without a doubt the sweetest kind of affirmation we are fortunate enough to ever get. It is very heartwarming to understand that people do acknowledge and internalize the positions we take to support and defend the Constitution and do understand the urgency and importance of the work we do. What may be unknown to many is that every single letter that we receive via email receives a personal, individual response. I am especially moved that the people who ask reasonably for clarification and understanding in good faith, or come with a stance that is filled with misinformation yet have open minds, are willing to assess logical reasoning and undisputed facts because logical reasoning is a process and the facts are disputed, at times, but only failingly so by ignoramuses who can't tell truth from fiction. Believe it or not, we get many of these letters, and we have helped many who write in, transforming them into true believers and supporters of the Constitution.

The last category of letters, the hate letters, is what I will never come to understand, no matter how long I live. I just cannot comprehend the hypocrisy and stupidity of these letters and the illogical reasoning they attempt to present. My brain fogs with shock and confusion when I read the blistering hate and pure viciousness they spew as they misunderstand our position and feel that we are personally attacking their beloved version of fundamentalist Christianity. The "kind, gentle, peace-loving" teachings of Jesus are tossed at us while they are simultaneously threatening highly specific and descriptive death and mayhem upon us. The incongruency of the two leaves me shaking. There is a disgusting underbelly to our civilization and the people responsible seem to think that it is perfectly okay to write this vitriol to me, my husband, my children and grandchildren, and our foundation staffers. Some are so "creative" in their stupidity that it would be laughable were it not so deeply dangerous and scary. It is of utmost importance to me that people like you understand the depth of the human side from which these letters attack. Be forewarned, many of the letters presented here are not for the faint of heart. They are personal, they are brutal, and they have forever affected and altered the course of existence for my entire family. So, when you read through these letters, you might be tempted to read them from a sarcastic point of view or as a joke of some sort. Perhaps the toughest point of view to read them from would be mine. Digest them as if you were me, as if it were YOUR family being subjected to these very same merciless attacks. Then you might begin to understand why I am presenting this book to you. I represent the human side, the softer side of the Foundation, and it's for myself and my family that they save the very "best" and most hate-drenched letters. Read this book as if you were a part of MY family, and you might begin to understand that, no matter how ridiculous and stupid they are, they are written by individuals whose faulty beliefs are only hardened by facts that stand in clear opposition to their treasured views of religious dominance and superiority. Now, how scary is that?

My husband tells me that life with him is like a day at the beach and my response is:

"Yes, dear, it is—in a tsunami."

IN THE BEGINNING...

The section headings in this book, along with the combined illustrations, have been created to relate to each chapter. They are homophobic, anti-Semitic, anti-Christian, Islamophobic, antiatheist, and racist. I certainly do not speak this way, believe in it, or condone this type of thinking. However, and very unfortunately, they represent the letters contained within each section very well. By far, the mildest chapter is where we begin.

Mikey and I created the Military Religious Freedom Foundation in 2005. In doing so, we had no idea the profound and dramatic changes this would bring to our lives.

In the frontier days of the Foundation's development, we were resolute, certain that what we were doing needed to be done. We had our supporters and those who stood firmly with us, but the amount of flak we took and where it came from was very surprising. We were barely a year or two into this fight when a reporter, who was interviewing me for an article, asked if I'd do it all again. I thought to myself, *What a silly question! Of course I would.* I remember her shaking her head as if she just heard me say something really stupid and wanted to clarify her question for me. I stood by my answer. It was the right

thing to do. We needed to do it, and so we did. Years later, I see her question for what it was underneath: concern for the safety and well-being of my family. So, would I do it again?

444.
July 26, 2013
Dear Mr. Weinstein,
Quite a nice scam you have going here. Kudos for inventing a problem that does not exist, creating a non-profit to "fix it", and soliciting $$$ from low-information sheeples. It is revolting and a sad commentary on our society that you are apparently succeeding.

The quote featured on your headline banner "When one proudly dons a US military uniform, there is only one religious symbol: the American flag. There is only one religious scripture: the American Constitution. Finally there is only one religious faith: American patriotism" is moronic on all levels. What blather! Our founders would be aghast that you distort the Constitution, the Bill of Rights, and equate belief in this country to a religious experience.

This is precisely what Islamists do and enforce. As a Jew, I find your misguided crusade an enormous embarassment.

Finally, do you really call yourself "Mickey"? Most kids grow out of the cute adolescent nickname by age 10 and adopt the more mature "Mike" or "Michael".

Grow up, get a real job and contribute something meaningful to society. This ain't it.

Regards

[name withheld]

defyljew

I will have to blame the Life® Cereal commercial and my mother for the reason my husband has the nickname "Mikey." When we were dating, my mother would fix dinner for us and any of Mike's classmates that were over at our house. Mike was a bit of a picky eater and had some very strong dislikes (no cheese, no butter, no onions, no mushrooms, no meatloaf, no casseroles…to name just a few). This had a tendency to frustrate my mother when she was trying to cook meals he would eat and enjoy. One day, when we were all standing around in the kitchen, my mother repeated what was being said on the Life® Cereal commercials at the time: "Oh, Mikey. He won't eat it. He hates everything!" Mike's classmates thought that was extremely funny, and so it began.

485.

October 24, 2013
Dear Mr. Weinstein
I am wondering whether during Holocust your relatives did not acknowledge and pray to GOD. Why taking such stupid stand about deleting the wow "GOD". What possible benefit except harm can come out of this?

Just to clarify, Jewish people believe in God. Most likely there were many prayers being said as they were shoved into the crematoria.

You may worship Money and fame , but wished you changed your name to avoid hatred toward fellow Jews and rising Anti Semettism .. The only people in the world other than some Jews who are supporting the state of Israel are Christian Rght. May GOD bless them, but assuredly your ancestors will be ashamed of you who from Abraham time believed in GOD as our creator..
Your organization and its aim is shameful. .
One day when you and or family member are experiencing near death situation, I am wondering who if any you will look up to.?

This is just a best guess based on my husband's

background and connection to his Jewish heritage. Even though he's very much a reluctant agnostic, I'm thinking Mikey will most likely pray to God in Hebrew as he's done ritually for years.

Hopefully for the sake of the welfare of Jews you stop with your unnecessary rhetoric .
Frankly I trust a GOD fearing person rather than an atheist.
Sincerely
[name withheld]

The assumptions being made here—and in all of the letters—are mind-blowing! Where on earth are these people getting this information?

575.
December 7, 2013
sounds to me like your organization is NOT for freedoms. Sounds like you want to make religion stand in the corner, and muzzle and bind those who practice it. And not let them have any say in the public arena. Aren't you using your own deeply held views to attack and constrain others who don't share your opinions? Sounds like you are using words to bend an shape the truth to your own liking. You are using a thin and fragile veneer of

"standing up for the oppressed" to justify your livid oppression and antagonism of religion. Sounds like you have an axe to grind.
[name withheld]

I don't know, but when I read this, it sounded more like fingernails on a blackboard than someone grinding an axe.

611.
December 12, 2013
Nobel Peace Prize??... hahaha Why would this falsely representing oranization truely believe they would ever, EVER receive the Nobel Peace Prize for being a Christian HATE group?? I almost spit my coffee out when I read the glorified "self" advertisment of being nominated for this reverned award as if that meant something. If that were the case, we might as well nominate the Ku Klux Klan for the Nobel Peace Prize as well as every other hate group in the United States!! LOL No.. you don't hate by race or culture.. but you hate and seperate by religion, hiding behind the trash you claim. I've even read on the front page of this organization's website, articles speaking out against Christians and praising themselves for accolades against them. As a United States Soldier, that this

organization proudly claims to represent, we the PEOPLE are presently at war with "hate groups" all over the globe.... Just because you hide behind the title of "Military Religious Freedom" doesn't fool us... We aren't sheep, we are the people of the United States of America. Find another hobby and let us have our freedom! "Don't Tread On ME"

[name withheld]

A hobby? Oh, my. If they ever had any idea of the amount of work...hobby, my ass. We have now, to date, been nominated six times for the Nobel Peace Prize. Please forgive the glorified self-advertisement of being nominated.

670.

March 12, 2014

Dear MRFF,

How dare you people make up a bullshit foundation to ridicule conservatives. At some point, all of you liberal douche bags have to sit and laugh at how stupid you really are. **We do?** It is beyond hilarious that people like you enjoy this kind of thing. **It is?** Why should he be punished? **Wait, what?** His rights have no been violated. **Who's he?** Maybe I will start a foundation to counter your foundation and so on and so forth.

Sounds like an interesting plan, but I'm not holding my breath.

It is disturbing that now it is all fine to suck dick and lick crotch in the military and everyone has to be fine with it, **Wait, they do? Is it really?** but heaven forbid a service member expresses their religion by their constitutional right **If they were expressing their religious views following the Constitution and in accordance with time, place, and manner, fine. What's the problem? Oh, yes. I know they don't seem to understand "time, place, and manner."** but some how it violates some pack of wild cry babies freedom. In 2016 your organization and others will undoubtedly be wiped from being a constant thorn in the happy existence of humans everywhere. I was ridiculed for being a straight white male from a religious family with money and never ran to the prinicipal when i was picked on or offended. Eventually the world will be normal again and it will not be a crime to be straight, love god and express it freely without persecution from the likes of you and other bleeding hearts who seek to control this country like hitler did. America was founded on god

and you would all be well to remember that rather than try to rid it from our history and bow to the muslim heretic in the white house.
[name withheld]

WHAT?!? Did that make any sense to anyone?

1677.
March 12, 2014
Disagree with everything you stand for. You are a charlatan and an sad man.
[name withheld]

"…and an sad man." *Sigh…*

I wonder from time to time about the quality of education I received growing up. My father was in the military and we moved around a lot. We lived in Greece when I was in first through fourth grades, and it wasn't until I was in the third grade that my father was able to get me into an English-speaking school on the base. I was behind the curve when it came to being able to read and write English, and I still struggle with spelling. Thank heaven for spell check. I guess many of these people who write in haven't yet discovered that feature on their operating systems.

26.
April 21, 2010
Military Religious Freedom Foundation:
Does anyone in your sick group need to be reminded that AMERICA was founded on Christian Religious Beliefs.
When in AMERICA the Islam need to follow Americans. If they could be upset – then get the hell out of AMERICA. If you are not Catholic and go to work in Rome do you think you would say that the POPE cannot hold a public prayer service?

All lands are welcome in AMERICA but do not try to change AMERICA to be their country. Maybe it would be best for your simple minded leader to move to be with the Islam people in their country and then have him tell them it upsets him to see them bowing to the east all the time and the Islam people must STOP that.

Get a grip on life or all of you should get OUT OF AMERICA.

What a bunch of cry baby whiners. You are disgusting, sick, and bottom dwellers. [name withheld]

Okay. Calling me, my husband, or any of us in the Foundation a bottom dweller is a low blow. So who, exactly, is the bottom dweller?

2.

April 22, 2010

I just heard that you asked to rescind the invitation to Franklin Graham to speak at the National Day of Prayer. WHAT ARE YOU THINKING?????? This great country is a Christian nation founded on Christian principles. THIS IS NOT A MUSLIM COUNTRY! What Franklin Graham said is true – Christians don't hate the Muslim people. We pray that they accept Jesus Christ as the

Son of God and their personal Savior. This is a CHRISTIAN COUNTRY! This is a volunteer event. The muslim people are NOT forced to attend. IF the Muslims at the Pentagon don't like it, they don't have to attend but DON'T ask to disinvite a great Christian leader to a National Day of Prayer for a CHRISTIAN NATION just to be "politically correct".
[name withheld]

Many letters come in after the Foundation has announced progress and victories that help balance and level the playing field between one religion and another and between religion and no religion. These letters often refer specifically to that particular issue that we were able to balance. Inevitably, all our letter writers were not happy with the outcome.

72.
April 26, 2010
Hey Hateful Christina Bigots,
Good luck in trying to take God out of the foxhole! I guess the hater who started this pathetic organization because he can't work and make a decent living....You produce nothing but hate......Nothing else....But let me know when you get God out of

the Foxhole!

1st Cav Division.......

Where God Goes!

If anyone is a bigot it is you , your husband or relative.

Do you have an issue with Christianity due to the fact you are Jewish, or just sad little atheist? My country was founded on religious principles and for you idiots not knowing who the enemy is , nor their religion, are just ignorant! Oh, the framers did not make this country or Republic per religion diversity but from government making all laws dealing with such...How do I know, my gggg was one of those framers. How dare you people judge our country and even Dr, Graham....You are the enemy within. You are the ones who are destructive to our country. We as a people or nation don't have to tolerate fanatics or a religion that calls for the death of non believers. Our country is a Christina nation and if you don't like it, get on a boat and leave the way yours came. Also, labeling people phobic is so third grade, try that crap somewhere else, because the majority of the country don't buy into that liberal bullshit.

The person who heads this sorry organization, you are a disgrace to the American Armed Forces and calling yourself an American. You are pathetic misguided hypocrites.

[name withheld]

I have learned a few things—a few rules of writing, you might say—that I didn't know before these letters started coming into our email boxes, and I thought I'd share them with you. If ever you get into a discussion with others and find that they don't necessarily believe the way you do, be sure to:

1. Yell certain points.

2. Resort to name calling early on. (Actually, that's the first thing you should do.)

3. Bring in talking points that have nothing at all to do with the issue at hand.

4. USE LOTS OF CAPITAL LETTERS!

5. Use random punctuation marks and lots of them!!!!!!!!!!!

6. If all else fails, personalize your attacks and resort to more name calling. Hell, call them everything you can think of!

81.

April 26, 2010

Mike, you are so off base. YOU want all Christians DEAD? I read your comments. YOU are what is wrong with this country. Are you closet Muslim? Do you hate our country so much? There was NEVER anything that said there was to be a separation of church and state!!!!!!! Just freedom to practice any religion. You want to force your evil views on all people. Yes Christians believe the Bible and for your information, you and your organization are helping fulll prophecy by condemning Christ and His followers. But, whether you believe or not, YOU are still going to burn in Hell!!!!!!!!!!!!!!!! I wish all you people would leave my country, (I am a native American, so I have every right to this country, YOU have zero rights to this land) People like you are ushering in Islam for everyone. I bet you voted for the pretender and chief, Obama the liar. Congratulations, you are anti-American, pro-evil, anti-Semitic, anti- Christian and just plain stupid. May God forgive you, for you know not what you do I will stand for Jesus and lay my life down for His word, me and 38 million other fanatics

Oh, and one more thing:
7. Speak like you know what the hell you are

**talking about. Forget about the real facts. They
only cloud the issue.**

2333.
March 23, 2011
Mr. Mickey Wienstien, my church and its fine
pastors, our congregation and my family and I all
wonder how you and your MRFF helpers sleep at
night? We have read the articles like the one in
last month's Nation magazine about you and your
wife and family and your Jewish-athiest MRFF.
You have singlehandidly disgraced America and its
Christian faith and culture and its Christian military. Whether you and your fellow evildoers accept
it or not, America IS a CHRISTIAN NATION as
it was always the ONLY plan of the founding fathers to be just that. Of course America's military
MUST be a Christian military because America
was always meant to be a CHRISTIAN nation. All
of the founding fathers such as Washington and
Adams and Franklin and Jefferson were devout
followers NOT of Islam or Judiism or athiesm but
of our Lord and Savior Jesus Christ. America is a
Temple to our Lord and Savior and you and your
MRFF trash dishonor and disgrace our American
Temple and its Christian military with lies from
Satan and secularists like a so-called separation of

church and state which is NOWHERE anywhere in the constitution. And you call yourself a lawyer? Other religions can be and exist in our CHRISTIAN America but only as long as they understand that they are NOT the real reason America shines like a Beacon of our Lord and Savior Jesus Christ on a Hill as President Reagan said. You are a just a Jew, as we have read in the newspapers and magazines, and are allowed to be a respectful guest in Christian America and you will be tolerated and safe, along with all the other false faiths and athiests as long as you understand who and what and where you stand in regard to America's Lord and Savior. Don't you understand that America's success in spreading the good news message of Christ to its citizens and to the world depends on our military to be its example and its messengers. End your furious battle against our Lord and surrender to His grace, spirit and guidance before it becomes too late. In Jesus' name, we will pray for you and your family and MRFF to stop or be stopped. 1 Corinthians 1:18

[name and location withheld]

643.

December 23, 2013

Dear Mikey,

Go to Israel, your true country. This country was founded by my ancestors and not yours. If you are uncomfortable with a Christian Country, Please leave. I participated in the 911 response and all that I saw was the rabbis arguing the Menorah should be higher than the Christmas tree on West end Ave. I did not observe any Jewish organizations offering their help during the crisis. However, I did observe many Christian volunteers and organizations helping out. In addition, there are very few Jewish men in our armed forces today.

As to the freedom of religion amendment. It was intended to prevent the establishment of a mandated religion similar to the Church of England. It was intended that the government not to prohibit the practice of religion in any form. This includes the display of Christmas Trees. I hereby promise that I will protest any Menorah that is placed on any publically owned land as long as your group is in existence. Once again , this country was established by Christians, who wanted a country free of religious persecution.

Menorahs are hocus pocus just like Christmas trees. The oil did not burn for 8 consecutive nights (it is tradition). Instead of being concerned of Christmas (Druid worship of nature) trees and nativity scenes; I would be concerned that because the liberals elected Obama; Iran may nuke Israel and the rest of the world. My family fought in the Revolution. I am proud to state that Nathan Hale and John Hancock are in my family tree along with many other heroes.

My wife is half-Jewish and my 4 children are Jewish by Jewish law. Her uncle (mother's brother)was at Bataan. My mother-in-law lost family in the holocaust. She did begrudge any religion and celebrated both holidays.

One day, people will take your religious persecution to the supreme court. You are no different than the KKK burning and bombing black churches in the south.

[name withheld]

2932.

January 30, 2014

Ya'll are horrible this nation was founded on God, and now that people have "feelings" everything has to change this world is going down. If you have stupid feelings you don't need to be in the military or go to war.

[name withheld]

679.
March 13, 2014
Dear Mikey,

Please change your name to the far more accurate, "Military Freedom From Religion Foundation." You, Mikey are a jerk. You're likely one of those ignoramuses that believe that Separation of Church and State is in the Bill of Rights. It isn't, the phrase appeared in a private letter from Thomas Jefferson and has been taken wholly out of context. Like it or not, Bud, we are a Christian Nation, always have been, always will be despite the likes of you. Get your heathen attitudes out of my military. BTW I did two tours in Vietnam. Were you even in the military? I doubt it. You're just another liberal asshole.

[name withheld]

Well, there you go. Forget everything you've ever learned from your history professors, for you have now been taught "correct" American history.

198.
September 8, 2011
Dirty jew Mikey, saw all about you on Fox News the other day and how you and your anti-American jew mrff foundation are trying to take the love and knowledge of Jesus out of our Air Force atom bomb missile training. Filthy stinking conniving merderous disloyal jew Mikey. everything you touch, jew boy, you corrupt. Go play with your arab raghead buddies and leave the Air Force nuclears and our Saviors blessings on how to launch them alone from your greedy bloody damn jew hands.
[name and location withheld]

Sixty-nine United States Air Force nuclear missile launch officers (sixty-one of whom were Christian), came to us and asked the Foundation to help stop this sort of training. They were able to provide us copies of the PowerPoint presentation slides that were used during the nuclear missile launch training. Thirty-four hours after we got ahold of this information, and jumped into action, the training was stopped. The Air Force had admitted to teaching the biblically-based "just war" theory as part of the official training for the past twenty years. However, with a bit of research, it was discovered that this biblically-infused training has been going on for twenty-five years or more. Within the United States Air Force nuclear missile launch officer community, this "just war" theory training was referred to as "Jesus Loves Nukes."

When I was growing up, I had no clue that people considered groups of people to be lesser or greater than the next person or any different than anyone else. In fact, it wasn't until I met Mikey that I realized how often people drew assumptions of ethnicity based on last names.

After people discover that our family is Jewish, they often proceed to make assumptions as to our intentions in forming the Foundation based on our ethnicity and religion. The "Jew bashing" that is presented here is just incredible to me. The writers may be attempting to address other issues, but these letters are so overwhelmingly anti-Semitic that they have been placed in this section. I am disheartened to have to say that this is the longest section in the book.

20.

Mikey,

So you anti-white anti-christian sheenie monkey, what do you pay yourself as president of your phonie tax dodging foundation? Typical yid money scheme. It would be interesting to see who your "contributors" are, wouldn't it? Why dont you reveal the directors' compensation?

53.

April 22, 2010

Mr. Weinstein:

Over the ages Jews are accepted then rejected. They are accepted as a minority group in a much larger population disrespect the values of the majority. The majority rejects the Jews sometimes with great violence, as happened in WW2.

What? I have read this far too many times and I still think, *What?*

Jews have an influence in this country way beyond their numbers. Their influence is becoming troublesome because they strive to diminish the prerogative of the majority to shape things how they see fit.

You don't like Christian centered organizations in the military, I dont have a problem with them. Your rant against Christianity is "uncivil and unwanted. Your rabid anti Christian crusade belies a Jewish infatuation to murder Christ again, like Jews did two thousand years ago.

It didn't go so well for the Jews the first time and it needs to be done again? Did I miss something?

The Jewish lobby that distorts American foreign policy protect Israel and organizations such as yours that attempt to derail the values of the majority weaken America, the country you claim to love. Your fear of Christians, who have been only kind,welcoming and protective of you, is disheartening.
Shame on you!
[name withheld]

I really didn't think that this was a kind and welcoming letter. So far, I'm not feeling the love!

4316.
September 1, 2010
Dominion is here jew-boy (and tools of the jews) get used to it. It will start on Wall Street (Jew

Street) and it will finish in Washington (Jewshington). Have a nice day JEW-BOY!

Wait...if it's here, hasn't it already started?

157.
March 3, 2011
Jews lie as naturally as they breathe, without even thinking about it.

"Thank you for being a voice for so many men and woman in the armed forces who are unable to speak out. "

Unable to speak out?! BS!! Who can shut them up?!

A jew decides to go to law school. What's new? He wants to "use the law", like you. An open admission of guilt. Another Christian hating jew. A religious jew no doubt, since everyone knows there is no such thing as race. Except the Talmud.

Feel The Hate
[name withheld]

Well, yes. I do feel the hate, the anti-Semitism, and the stupidity!

163.

March 21, 2011

listen up, fuck you jew-boy Mikey trayter; you and your Jesus hating band of anti American MFRR scum can try all you want to keep our lord and savioyer's love of christyan power out of our USA Army but you will fail as you all are of the evil demon devil and always have been   you try to stop us from bringing His grace and love to the rest of the world with the USA armd forces and especially to the arab raghead and camul jockeys and our King of kings will open can of whup ass on you MFRR jew bastrds as He has done to punihs Japan and theyr false religyuns   you will all burn in hell anyways for your evilness to fight Jesus in the USA Army!

I have to keep reminding myself that they are trying to bring "Grace" and "Love" to everyone.

3941.

May 12, 2011

aw, too bad that mikey the kikey doesnt like the Wash Times calling the Air Forces Academy's freak religins exactly what they are, FREAK Religons? of course because hes a piece of shit jew filth trying to hide behind the constittusion so he can

be of his true coniving Savior killing jew nature. And demon-clever lawyer away all of our Christian rights out of our Christian country and Christian army, navy, air force and marines founded by Christians FOR Christians and BY Christians. kikey mikey doesnt like it? MFRR doesnt like it? it doesnt matter since you will all burn in hell for murdering the USA savior Jesus Christ who is not a freak religiun unlike jews and islams and hundis and buddists and athists and all the other homo freaks you try to replace peaceful American Christians with. mikey the kikey mikey the kikey mikey the kikey mikey the kikey see you soon
[name withheld]

Okay, then. That was well said and well written. I'm especially fond of the way the word "religion" was spelled in so many different ways.

179.
August 3, 2011
MRFF:
Die you fucking jews

Why do all you Jews always get expelled from every Country that lets you in? You're a fucking minority in America, most Americans are Christian, if you

don't like that then go get gassed or go something else you fucking kike.
Sooner or later it's a reality, Don't you love how America is waking up to all your little tricks. You think you won be will def have the last laugh kike.
[name withheld]

I got lost. What is the reality?

4419.
October 3, 2011
Dear MRFF:

jewboy Mikey Whiningstein uses his endless jew money to buy a roadway sign in the streets near the Air Force Academy to show a message from another jewboy General shwartz who heads up the air force to force the hand of a good man, a folower of the Lord Jesus Christ, General Guold. To send out the first General's message to try to stop the brave Christian General Guold who heads up the Air force's academy from trying to save the souls of lost jews and athiest and all the others who are lost to satan at this academy. Funny isnt it. Just look deep enough whenever anyone tries to stop the spread of the word of Jesus and you will always find a disesed jew like mikey whinerstein and his jew loot and his master satan.
[name withheld]

I do not think that the following writer understands that Jews do not celebrate Christmas. Jewish kids typically don't have manger scenes and Christmas toys, but there I go, again, trying to use those pesky facts.

273.
December 20, 2011
Dear MRFF,

its always you low dirty jews, mickey who spoil it all for the rest of humanity. killing and selling out our Lord and Savior Jesus Christ was never enough for your demonic breed. no, you have to take manger scenes away from our troops on their bases and Christmas toy away from inocent kids at the air academy. we see that you have kids too. what would you do to a jewboy who took their manger scenes away and took the Christmas toys away too? what will Jesus do to you, jew? your just a lovely tool of satan as are all jew trash. but you jew mickey are satans special favorite. which is why you are the numer one enemy of our Lord and savior Jesus Christ. you will lose jew mickey. you will lose everything.
[name and location withheld]

232.
November 5, 2011
Dear MRFF:

How a Jew can say it is too Christian? That what he
is ,,no? Mikey Weinstein..
No wonder there is antisemitism in USA...because
of Jews like him. Jews like Mikey Weinstein are the
reason...
[name withheld]

There is not a single complete sentence in this letter.

252.
November 10, 2011
Dear Mikey Weinstein,

Typical stinking jew boy Mikey to try to stop the
love of Jesus to bring toys to needy children who
will burn forever in the Lake of fire (like jewboy
mikey will for sure) unless they are saved by the
grace of Jesus and Franklin Graham's Xmas gift
shoeboxes. whats the matter jewboy mikey? you
don't like little kids getting Xmas presents from
the Air academy cadets because their are lessons
about why they must be saved from certain hell by
only Jesus tucked inside the shoe boxes for their

education? Too bad jewboy scum. fuck you jewboy scum. you will burn in hell jewboy scum with all your other jew scum burning with you for what you did to our Lord and savior and what you still try to do to this very day jewboy mikey. if you had only been born a few years earlier. Hitler would have taken care of you but good so you could no longer attack Jesus and the little children the Air Academy cadets are only trying to help Jesus save from the hell you will burn in forever. Oh I do love the smell of jewboy mikey burning in the morning. fuck you jew mikey. Fuck you jew family and your jew slut wife and jew mongrel ofspring and fuck your jew MFRR. I pray to Jesus that your heart will explode and bleed out gushing through your pointy jew nose. Jesus and the Air Academy will have the last laugh while you choke to death on your own blood you evil jew scum fucker.
[name withheld]

The previous letter, along with the following letters, are so filled with hate and vitriol and some of the worst anti-Semitism that I have read, that I offer no further comments in this delightful chapter. Do I need to mention that they are also some of the stupidest statements and/or arguments in this entire book?

335.
May 14, 2012
Dear Mikey,

we known many things about you mikey. we know you love the arab muslem sand niggers and hate Lord Jesus and Christians. We know you are a kike jew lawyer with a big mouth and uppity attitude. we know the commie pinko reporters write whatever you tell them to write because you are a doomed jew prick. and we know where you live and travel and everything. and we know you hate America which is a nation founded up on Jesus our Savior PERIOD. Poor Kikey Whineshit now you scream and howl about our brave Army teaching the only answer to islam sand niggery. Which is to drop nukes on muslems cities and the terorists living there which is all the populations weather they be islam children or grown ups its all the same. all muslems are terorists its in there blood. just like jewblood loves only money and betraying trechery as you framed and murdered Jesus. you just can't help yourself jewboy Kikey. Any more than the muslems can. blood does as blood does. Nuke All The a-rabs Now should be our Army's battle cry and no. 1 order of there day. Which it was fine and dandy until you shoved your big jew nose into there war business. The Army has it right and now you try to stop it? you don't have long and you won't. It is always comforting to know as a patriotic American Christian that you will burn forever in the fire ovens of hell in unending torture with your muslem scum pals and your Military Religous Foundation fools and your ugly Whineshit kike wife and jew piglet children.

[name withheld]

Okay, wait! I know I said, "No further comments from me," but this just has to be revisited: "It is always comforting to know as a patriotic American Christian that you will burn forever in the fire ovens of hell in unending torture with your muslem scum pals and your Military Religous Foundation fools and your ugly Whineshit kike wife and jew piglet children." Really?

347.
June 3, 2012
Dear Mikey,

saw you in our texas paper today crapping on our savior His nation of America and those of us who follow Him, jewboy. maybe you should look around this fallen country and this lost world and see that it is only by surrendering to Christ as his slave of mercy and obedience that any of us will be spared the bloodbath to come thanks to your lord satan.

and you would take Jesus away from our soldiers? you try to hide behind a damn piece of paper the constitution. more jew lawyer tricks. there are no Godly freedoms there in that old paper in washington museum. try though you might you will lose, jew. read your New Testament bible before it is too late, jew. it is probably already too late for you and your black evil MRRF anyway. Im glad of it. we will be seeing you around. we are many.
[name and e mail address withheld]

365.
July 5, 2012
mickey=jew lawyer=internasional kike=Jesus hater=america hater=islam lover=the grave
[name withheld]

5012.
May 8, 2013
Mike Weinstein,
These acts of redefining tolerance by coming against religious rights of Christians in the military is so upsurd, rediculous, and immoral. You shame yourself as a Jew and mis-represent Jews, and the God of Yisrael, and Yisrael itself. Christians support and bless Yisrael and the Jews and is this how you reward them. You are acting in darkness and you are

showing there is nothing good in you in this hateful intolerant action with the Pentagon. This will shorten your life. I am a practicing Jew and was a part of the US Air Force. I am sick and see parallels with Hitler in what you are doing. I guess you love Hitler and intend to imitate him. That is a very shameful thing for a so-called Jew. Are you a new Hitler? Turn around before the same judgement he had comes upon you.

[name withheld]

418.
May 12, 2013
Dear Mr. Weinstein,
your a fucking barking dog jew weinstien. you and your little group of mffr queers are all jews. one and all. includin jewbassador jew wilson. and col. lawrense wiljewerson who is the house nigger of that niggerjew colin powell. you all have no right to stop our armies from being the warriors for Christ. for which our christian nation was formed. for Christians. by Christians and only Christians. meant to spread the gospel of The Lamb to the world held prisoner by jew killers and there international fellow travelers. we know what you want mickey The Big Jew weinstien. and your evil jew blood and the animal blood of your family and

friends will be spilt by the counless gallons in vain. we will laugh with the Lord as the Christ slaughters all of you. hitler was the only one to stand up to your jew filth. He saw you subhumans for what you are. we who follow the Christ will never let you win for the devil. America's armies live and fight for The Word of the Christ. praise the Lord Jesus who will finish what hitler started. you have no chance and no prayer.
[name withheld]

463.
August 12, 2013
i never heard of this communist marxist jewish organization and there lots of these organizations now ..filthy little fagot kikes who head them up like they head up the nigger naacp...this following organization is pointedly obvious that weinstein is a filthy shitkike and seeks to further the lubavitch agenda against whites and christianity and islam is getting a pass on this shit ..the name allah can be used and praying or thanking jesus in school or track meet or military will get you in trouble ...
The MRFF is a very insidious organization. It is headed up by a man named Mikey Weinstein. He has called Christians "human monsters" and "enemies of the United States Constitution".

Weinstein is convinced that sharing the gospel of Jesus Christ while in the military is "sedition and treason" and should be punished as such. You would think that people like Weinstein would be dismissed as lunatics, but unfortunately under the Obama administration he has been brought in as a special adviser to the Pentagon. What a crazy world that we live in. ..

its not funny but it is preposterous that the enemy of mankind ,the jew says christians are monsters when oit was the jews who killed 70 million white russians after the bloody coup in russia 1917 ..it was the jews who have committed every genocide against wghites since esther and cypress and romans in 117 ad to 200,000 people ..france revolutio was jews ...the irish starvation holocaust committed by kike disraeli pm of britain (5 million irish perish)...civil war 700,000 total kia from both sides ......slavery and the death of hundreds of thousands of whites who were slaves as well as niggers during the slave years ....1915 armenian 4.7 million nkiled by jews ..1936 bolshevik kikes rolled into spain and murdered 2.5 million women children and priests and they tried to stain franco with this shit but it was jews ..the genocide of germany dressed up to look like ww2 ..40 million germans dead ..1940 -1955 includes ethnic germans from checkos yugoslav poland pows def's ..etc orphans ..sachenhausen camp where commmisars killed 700,000 germans ..i only heard about the 14,000 german teenagers the jews torured and killed there and buried them on the property ..they are still there ..the jews have always maintained a ludicrous statement that germans killed 700,000 russians there ..and then they said it was jews ..or maybe they meant russian jews ..if so ,good ..but its the old lie where wehn the jews hurt you they scream in pain ..

this MRFF shit is so off the charts and to claim christians hate the constitution is a big lie that no one believes anyway ...this guy needs to be shut down and all communist kikes like him ..if we dont get creative and busy we will suffer the same fate as many other nations who are and have been under the control of murderous jew communists and their rabbis ..

2817.
November 12, 2013
Date: November 12, 2013 at 5:05:37 PM MST
To: ——@militaryreligiousfreedom.org
Subject: Dirty FUCKING KIKES!!!!
All you evil low life serpent KIKES will never win!!!!

609.

December 12, 2013

Hey jewboy Mickey Whinerstein. The Air Force Base in S. Carolina should make a nativity scene out of your dismembered fucking body parts. You stinking kike commie athiest liberal dick sucking Obummer loving Jesus hating faggot lawyer. Who worships satan queers and abortions and muslum sand niggers like Obummer more than your own country. TRAITOR JEW!

661.

January 28, 2014

Hey Kikey Whinersteen. It figures you'd go on a TV show hosted by filthy stinking muslem arabs like Cenk Uyger (notice stupid non-American name). You and him fooled no true Americans. None.

He sucked your perverted curcumsized dick real good for you on TV. Didn't he Kikey? The only things uglier than your and Cenks faces are your skank wives. You and Cenk must be pitiful hard up. 2 uglier women then your squaws there are not. What you expect of she-kikes and she camel-jockeys?

Oh and Nice try crucifying our savior Jesus Christ again and again on the A-rab's TV show. It's all a hellbound hebe like you would know anyway. Can't you get it threw your jew head that America's armed forces are designed to be of The Christ and for The Christ. And only The Christ? The military's Mission is to kill the rag heads. Convert the jewboys and jewgirls or kill them too. Liquidate the fags and queers. And terminate the abortionists and socialists. Nuke em all.

Your days are numbered Kikey Whinersteen. Too bad you were born too late for the crematory camps.

Christ returns soon. His kingdom come Thy will be done. America's armed forces are Christ's right hand.

Stop your jew war on Jesus The Christ in the military now. you will not be warned again.

We pray for your long and painful children's deaths. They are drench in the blood of your sins. Suffer as you make Christ Jesus suffer you fucking kike.
On your knees to The Christ NOW!
Do it, Kikey! Heil Hitler!
[name withheld]

for the only true Lord and Savior. He who will soon return to lay vengeance on your blackness. And He with our spirit filled Christian US of A military will destroy you and your evil family of demon followers. By Jesus hand you will soon be cast into the pits of your jew home in hell. To burn forever and ever screaming in pain. Rejoice in the Word! kikey wienstein's Day of Judgment draws near.

John 8 and verse 44 You belong to your father, the devil, and you want to carry out your I object to your organization's What a bunch of bullshit What a bunch of bullshit What a bunch of bullshit father's desires. He was a murderer from the beginning, not holding to the truth, for there is no truth in him. When he lies, he speaks his native language, for he is a liar and the father of lies.

Revelations 20 and verse 10 And the devil, who deceived them, was thrown into the lake of burning sulfur, where the beast and the false prophet had been thrown. They will be tormented day and night for ever and ever.
[name withheld]

1012.
From: my63mustang@jefdayvuslives.com
Subject: you fucking piece of shit jew

Date: August 21, 2014 at 6:09:03 PM MDT
To: Information Weinstein <mikey@militaryreligiousfreedom.org>

jewboy don't you evercome back to our state. Your not wanted here. Keep you godam mffr hands off our Holy Univ. of No. Georgia Cadets corps. you fucking jew muslam queer loving jew. servant of satan. Why don't you eat some of your jewbread soked with the blood of innocent Christian children? To make it tasty for you you jew of jews. We don't eat your jew children wienstein. How you like it if we eat your jew children wienstein? Our church met last night to disgust all about you right here in our back yard in Ga. We all hope you choke to death eating your little piece of jewbread. Then burn for all ages in hell. Jesus Christ Rules and His Kingdom Come at UNG Corps!

3193.
April 1, 2014
Because he is a devil loving Christian hating, fag loving muslum loving, America hating, military hating athiest commie leftist with a big jew mouth an uppity jew anarchist socialist attitude. Fire up the ovens boys!
[name withheld]

THE FIELD GENERAL OF THE GODLESS ARMIES OF SATAN

When reading these letters, I start with the assumption that coherent thoughts and arguments may be offered. However, given the name of this section, don't expect very much in the way of coherence here.

38.
BTW don't you just love the way jews nowadays try to blame the Romans exclusively for crucifying our Lord? Traditional Christian teaching is that Pilate saw no blame in Jesus and washed his hands of the matter. Like a bureaucrat, he defered to the jews themsekves to decide Jesus fate. This is the doctrine which jews oppose and call hateful and anti-Semitic. You are against God and have NO special dispensation from Him. Dumbass Zionist Christians are misguided tools. Can you say Satan?

Hell, yes. I sure can!

172.
June 15, 2011
Our nation and it's soldiers yearn for the sweet and nurturing love of Christ Jesus. And only our Savior, to give us the military might and leadership to smite Satan and the gays and the Lord of Lies' moslem and atheist armies of evil. This clever judas lawyer

Weinstien's real father is Satan. It is the Word of our Lord. And his witch wife and demon spawn children are too of Satan (John 8:44). And MFRR henchmen are as well. They all so eagerly fly to stand in direct conflict with our Son of Man, Christ Jesus. They are of Darkness. They fight only for islamist and atheists and queers and false Christians. They fight for Satan. But our Lord is an awesome Lord. Every true American citizen soul to Jesus in this Land of the Free and the Home of the Brave will rejoice and feast when our Lord hurls judas Weinstien and his hosts to there second deaths into the depths of the Fire Lake of eternal damnation. (Revelation 20:14) As it is written it shall be done.
[name withheld]

There is a sentence fragment in the letter above that refers to "false Christians." It seems that a large chunk of our Christian clients would fit into the "false Christian" category according to the person that wrote this particular letter. Way to judge!

173.
June 22, 2011
Know Jesus, know Peace. No Jesus, no peace. Know Weinstein, know satan. No Weinstein, no satan. (Colossians 2:15)
[name withheld]

The person who sent in this letter knows the difference between the word "know" and the word "no" and how to use them. Yay! He does not, however, understand sentence structure.

282.

January 6, 2012

Our church prayer group hope that Mikey and his band of Christ haters at the Military Religious RAPE Foundation, mrff are finally happy that they have won their war for satan at the Air Force Academy. Because of this one alone horrible man and the evil horde he leads all of the goodness of the Word from Jesus has been removed from the cadets. Is it any wonder that rapes are happening? And more evil is surely on its way there. this is what Mikey wants. Thanks to Mikey and his sick diciples. world history shows that any time you remove the Word of the Savior from the people than satan's demons rush in. But satan cant do this without his leutenants of darkness. which Mikey and the mrff hordes are. ok, do you see that mikey is the worst rapist there is. He and his black army rape the Word of the Christ from where our American leaders wanted it all along next to the heart and harth of every good citizen. This is specialy true for our military. And what should we do

to rapists like Mikey? No Jesus No Peace. Know Jesus Know Peace. No mikey no mrff and no rape no satan.
[name withheld]

So sweet.

305.
February 19, 2012

Dear Military Religious Freedom Foundation,

Christians are sweet, loving, gentle, caring, spirit-filled spreaders of the light of our Lord and Savior Jesus Christ and, thus are blessd with eternal life.
Mikey Whinstein the jew-lawyer and his evil MRFF demons are sour, hateful, brutal, callous, satan-filled sewers of the darkness of the Devil and, thus are condemned to eternity in the fires of hell.
[name withheld]

So says the sweet, loving, gentle, especially caring and spirit-filled author of this letter.

350.

June 11, 2012

be sure to send a nice card to your daddy satan for fathers day this sunday, mickey. he must be so proud of the work you his favortie son and you fellow slaves to satan do to weakin America by destroying her armies at your mfrr. Christ see it all and your time to pay is fast approaching (John 3:36).

8714.

June 24, 2012

There is no reason I can conjure that you would take it upon yourself to eradicate religion from the Armed Forces other than the fact that you are surely working for the Antichrist.

Though that may seem preposterous to some, it does not to you because you and I both know the truth. Know this Satan, in the end you will ultimately fail.

[name withheld]

I was tempted to mark this next letter up with red ink because of this ironic challenge: "I am an American and a college graduate... This e-mail will contain no misspellings or gram-

matical errors or profanity as you often receive in your so-called hate mail." There were just too many corrections, though, and I was concerned that it would be difficult to read the actual letter, which is pretty amazing.

366.
July 23, 2012
Mr. Mikey Weintein,

I am an American and a college graduate. I have a wife and children. I just finished reading your book. I am very active in my church, We are all believers in the truth that Jesus Christ as the sole Lord and Savior of fallen mankind. (John 14:6) The men in my church have been closely observing the fiendish activity of your Military Religioius Freedom Foundatiuon for some time now. We have seen the negative messages sent to you and your family and the MRFF. This e-mail will contain no misspellings or grammatical errors or profanity as you often receive in your so-called hate mail. As you can see I am an educated man with a profession requiring intelligence. This communciation will, however, beg you to disband immediately your black foundation as it is both unGodly, unChristian and unAmerican. I know that you do not believe that satan is real. But he is and you and your wife and children and the Military Religious Freedom Foundation and all of those who support it are either willing or ignorant slaves to the Dark One. We do not yet know which but we will find out soon. It doen't really matter as you are all responsible for the evil you spread by trying to drive Christianity out of the armed services. All of you, especially you, Mr. Weinstein, as the charismatic and clever ring leader must stop your wickedness immediately and suit up to fight off your Master who is satan. (Ephesians 6:11) You have opened wide the door to the devil by denying America's Chrisitan priorities of State. Your blasphemous "success" has grown steadily more dangerous as you rush so hard to work to deny Christ his rightful presence and prominence in our nation's military. You have opened the door wide, wide, wide Mr. Weinstein for your ecstatic master, satan. Last Friday he bought a ticket to see the Batman movie in Colorado. Courtesy of you and your fellow travelers of pro-abortion, no guns allowed, judges get to decide everything and muslims are as good as Christians. And gays are "born that way". And the U.S. is a "secular" nation where Christianity is just another "religion option" for our troops and the lost peoples of the many countries they are fighting in. How ignorant you are. Can you not see that if you take away Jesus there is a void which will happily be filled, and is filled, by satan? The blood of that movie theater is on all of your hands. Cease and desist, Mr Weinstein. Let Christ replace satan in your still beating heart. (Matthew 7:8)

666.
July 10, 2013
mikey cannot wait until your made dead and punted to hell by The Lamb where youll burn forever for foursaking Jesus' love for you and for keeping our army under spell of your father satan. very soon now. oh and we pray your whole famly and the mfrr is made dead by The prince of Peace and also burn with you naked in hell for time imemorial

Wow. All of this being asked of The Lamb and The Prince of Peace. I wonder, is this one entity or two separate entities doing the stripping and the burning? There seems to be a bit of an incongruency here.

473.
September 25, 2013
I am a proud Christian living and spreading The Word of our Lord and Savior Jesus Christ here in

Tulsa. Me and my wife came to listen to the devil's own Mikie Wienstein at the All Soul's unitarian church here last saturday. Our pastor told us the next day at Sunday Service that this so called "church" should be renamed as "All Soul's Going To Hell" for 2 reasons. First it invited one of the greatest enemys of Christ wienstein to even speak here in Tulsa in the first place. Second because noone at that "church" has been saved by the blood of the Lamb Jesus Christ. And they all then will burn in the Lake of Fire for they rejection of our Savior. We listened to mikie Wienstein speak his evil words against allowing Christ to impower our U.S. army soldiers. We watched the jews face. We could not help but notice his face. Being a cunning jew he has a shrewd jew face to begin with to confuse the people. But the spirit on that dark face of his could only be of the Dark One himself satan. It was so obvious. It gave my wife and me chils to behold his demonism. My wife wanted to ask him a question at the microphone about him being of satan. But his evil glare from his dark father the fallen angel satan kept her from the strength to do so. And it was useless anyway. As all the others there will burn erternally in hell with that jew of satan. And he had to bring his big nigra guards with him for protection? He has no protection

from The Way, The Truth and The Life of Jesus. Mikie should no that there is no protection from those who kiss the lips of satan. And reject the free gift of the love of Christ. He gets what is coming for him from the warriors of the Savior. It is only a matter of time now.
[name withheld]

I'm just a little curious here. If my husband is Satan, does that make me Mrs. Satan?

641.
December 21, 2013
Dear Mikey,
Nothing.
Watched you cast your evil spell on Bill Oreilly.
Whole world saw it.
And now knows you for what and who you really are "Mikey".
Satan pure and simple. You are evil incarnite.
[name withheld]

What I saw while watching the Bill O'Reilly segment to which this person refers, was Bill O'Reilly making a COMPLETE and TOTAL ASS of himself with no help from either Mikey

or Satan. Please forgive the capital letters/ shouting, but I am merely following the rules I outlined in "Our Christian Nation."

I find I'm in need of quoting Rodney King here: "Can't we all just get along?" I wish that we could. The world would be a much kinder place.

3.

I want to send my help to your organization, by volunteering to help you burn down churches. Especially nigger chruches. You are a fucking idiot!! The only reason that we have been so blessed by GOD is because we were founded on christian principles!!! I CURSE you to fail and die a VERY severe death mikeyweinstein!!!!!   I hope all your kids turn out gay as hell, take it in the ass, and get aids and die!!!!! Die Fag

12.

Submitted via our volunteer webform...

First Name: You

Last Name: Willdie

Email Address: youareapolesmoker@tryingtokillamerica.com

I would like to volunteer to:

        x I have this great way I can help -

                     By killing Christians on sight, that's what you want right?

Military Background: 1st Brig General

Education Background: I learned how to fuck at your moms house
Current Job: Plotting the death of mikey weinstein...... nah, just playing,,,,, or am i??
Special Talents: I can kill a dolphin from 1000 yards
Areas of Interests: Killing gays, killing liberals, killing fags, killing in general
Religious Preference: I believe God will curse you to die for working for such a horrible company!!!

301.
February 15, 2012
Fucking liberal faggots! Those Marine snipers let you jerk off in the comfort of your warm bed while you complete your fetish with your dog!
[name withheld]

9946.
May 19, 2012

Dear MRFF,

MIkey doesn' like "it"? Mikey doesn't like it when real Americans stand up to Muslum murderers and liars. Mikey doesn't like it when real Americans say that all the Muslums are murderers and liars,

which they are, young and old, male and female because their so-called "faith" require it of them. Mikey doesn't like it when our top military schools and military leaders tell us that to protect the world from these murdering and lying smelly creatures that we need to use nuclaer weapons on them and destroy them all before they and their do it to us. Mikey also doesn't like it when real Americans say that queers should not be allowed to serve in the military or to mary other queers. Mikey doesn't like it when he told that the real America is a nation of devot Chrsitians and that was the way it has been from the beginning. Mikey doesn't like that real Americans are lovers of Jesus Christ not haters of our Lord like Mikey is. Oh Mikey says that many "Chrsitians" support him and his fake foundasion group of MRRF. But when you look at Mikeys "Christians" it's a funny thing that they are not true followers of our Savior at all. Funny thing about Mikey is that he's a jew. yes a clever jew and that says it all. Real Americans are not jews and real Americans know how the muslims have to be eliminated and real Americans know that the faggots deserve no safe and respect and especially not in the army of America. How do we get through to Mikey and his false prophet group of MRRF. same way we get through to the muslims and the queers.
[name withheld]

382.
February 21, 2013
Dear Mr. Weinstein,

you love the fags so much at the air academy jewboy whydon't you just try fucking yourself. To see
why Jesus said that faggots should be stoned to
death. you and your whole family and your mfrr
tribe should all be too.
[name withheld]

658.
January 2, 2014
May our Lord and savior sweep all of you away to
you rightfull places burning in hell eternal. Starting with Mickey Weinstein. Who loves the fags
muslems and jews more than he loves America
and its people. May the new year bring Jesus wrath
upon you all.
[name withheld]

735.
July 18, 2014
We drove through you spic infested town of wet
backs yesterday. Had the windows down. So we
could smell the mixture of your kike stink and
demon shame. on you and you're she kike bitch

cripple wife. You try to bring your father satan to destroy our soldiers jewboy? No way. The Word shall defeat you. And lay you in ruins for eternity. But it is we who shall destroy you for the glory of Christ. You are death and will be destroyed by The Lamb. 1 Corinthians 15:26

6652.
August 11, 2014
Served 25 plus years in this MANs Army. My nephews still do. We made history by beating the faggots and queers to raw meat. Kicking shit out of sand niggers and hajis in the Gulf war. The faith that shows us in the Army how to win is only one. Jesus Christ period. Hope your happy helping homos and a-rabs destroy America you jew bait Weinstein. You say you help 'Christians' but only the ones who are fucking scared to stand up for Jesus Christ. Where it counts. Which is everywhere. You want a-rab raggity heads and fudge packers leading our military? Only thing worse would be womans and jews. Course all jews are women anyway.

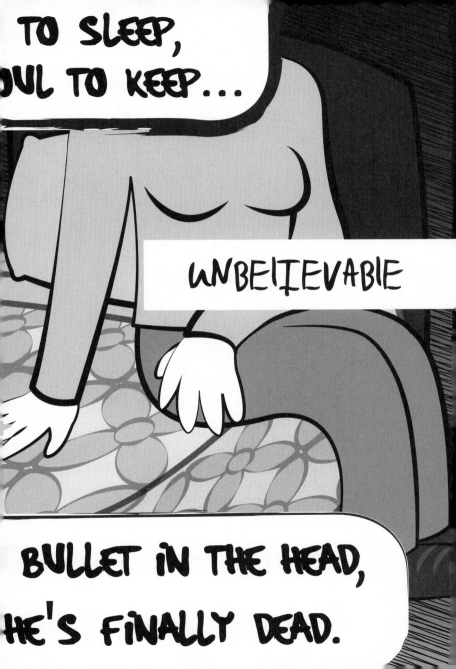

Most of the letters we get can easily be categorized into more than one chapter here. It's a difficult task, though, to figure out exactly where they best belong. There are also the misfits—the letters that don't fit neatly into any specific category, but definitely need to be included. After choosing this selection of letters, it was obvious we had many misfits on our hands. I decided to reread the letters and let them tell me what chapter to put them in. I happened to be reading these letters with my publisher and, letter after letter, I kept repeating a single word in my head. When I finished the last letter, I looked over, and my publisher said that very word. I have a sneaking suspicion that this very same word will come to you. Here, in this chapter, I present to you, the unbelievable.

7.
OUR HISTORY TEACHES US THAT AMERI-
CA CAME TO BE BECAUSE OF PEOPLE ES-
CAPING RELIGIOUS OPPRESSION. YOUR
ORGANIZATION WANT TO OPPRESS AND
SUPRESS RELIGION. YOU ARE ABOUT
AS ANTI-AMERICAN AS THE TALIBAN. IT
SEEMS THAT THE BEST DNA FROM YOUR
FATHER RAN DOWN YOUR MOM'S LEG,
AND THE BAD DNA STAYED PUT. WITH
PEOPLE LIKE YOU, OUR COUNTRY WILL
BE LUCKY TO SURVIVE.
[name withheld]

36.
just watched the clip you have posted on your web
site .Are you for real preaching about Jesus Christ
is a threat to are national security? Youre out of
your friggin mind you hate jesus soo much your
foaming out the mouthwith this garbage your
spewing. the national security threat is some piece
of shit trying to stamp out religion in the armed
forces your the ones that should be locked up. con-
spiring with the muslim news media to stamp out
christianity. I'll bet if they were trying to convert
them to be jewish we would not hear a peep from
you but we all know the muslims would rather die

than become jewish and you cant stand the fact that someone might decide to follow jesus ohh that would be terrible. well know this after every rotten thing youre trying to do jesus still loves you. in spite of youre being a traiter and a big pile of shit. have a nice day p.s. your org. should be named anti religious freedom because that youre real mission no matter waht you try and pass yourself off as bill the christian

[name withheld]

80.

April 26, 2010

All I have to say is you are lucky you have one of your own in the White House. Osama Obama did not fool all of the people. I for one despise the bastard. Additionally, I say that Allah goes down on little boys and grown men, on the guise of getting them to kill them selves and get 72 virgins......All he wants is fresh meat.

Allah is a sick dog........and your religion represents dogs as well

[name withheld]

175.
July 5, 2011
KIKEy Weinstein, ambASSador Joe Wilson, Mike-
The Kike Lover-Farrell, Ed ASSner and Reza ASS-
lan. Unhappy Forth of July. None of you are real
Americans. You will all burn for all eternity in hell-
fire. John 3:36
[name withheld]

1285.
August 4, 2011
Dear Mr. Mickey Mouse:

Short, bald, impotent, cowardly, paranoid atheist.
(oh, I almost
forgot-with tiny feet!-I can only be embarrassed for
you at the thought of
your equally infinitesimal pecker!–short jews are
infamous for stubby
units) What's shorter than a jew's prick?...a black
man's to-do list!!
[name and location and employer's name withheld]

386.
March 29, 2013
Dear Mr. Weinstein,
Every Easter for the past few years a member of our
ladies church group is asked to contact you. She

has demanded that you cease and desist from further crucifying our Lord and Savior Christ Jesus. And every year you reject the demand. You are a stiff necked jew (Exodus 32:9). And you just keep on crucifying The Christ. You crucify Him by your public denials. You deny, deny, deny. You deny that America is and always has been founded only as a Christian Nation. You deny that our American military is designed to further the Gospel of the Lord. For sake of all the world. You deny that our soldiers can be offerred The Gift of salvation buy their military leaders. You deny that the arabs in afghanistan Iran, Iraq and Kuwait shall be presented with The Word of Christ. With tender love by our Christian soldiers. We know your a jew. In America even jews, atheists and muslems are tolerated to be citizens. But not if they do not allow American Christians the fair chance to save them. From their false faiths. From an eternity in Hell with satan. A fair chance is all we ask you, Mickey and MRRF. Its right there in the constitution. You deny that too. You say your a lawyer so you should know this. Noone stops our soldiers from being saved more than you. So they're blood is on your hands. We have told you this. You don't care. Your in league with satan and will suffer for that in Hell for eternity. It is too late for you. You are a cowardly detestable sorcerer. Your second death is assured. (Revelations 21:8). Jesus The Christ commands you to hell. But you have a wife and children. We have all their pictures. And we pray on them for their salvation. That it is not too late for them. We ask you to think of your family. In order to stop you from fighting the Gospels spread in our military. And to the arabs in Arabia. And even the godless in Korea. Mickey fights and denies Christ to our troops. satan smiles. Jesus bleeds. At least see your family saved from your fate in the Lake of Fire. You are a deceiver and slave to satan (Revelations 20:10

395.
May 1, 2013
Dear Mikey,
I find your hate filled organization repugnant. You would not dare spill such hate filled bile against muslims, you know better. But you have found your target against Christians who will not, no, cannot fight back.

Who the hell does he think he's kidding with that statement? "But you have found your target against Christians who will not, no, cannot fight back." From what I understand, every single letter in this book comes from

self-professed "Christians." If these letters aren't a form of fighting back, then I don't know what is.

I have never seen such bile filled hate in my life except out of other extremist groups such as the KKK or the Black Panthers.

Or the letters compiled here in this book.

Is this the tack of your group. Target Christians to raise money and express your hatred and drive Christians out of the military? Do you have a hammer and nails at the ready for when you and your marxist comrads have your opportuntiy to round up Christians and nail them to crosses once again or feed them to wild beasts?

God save of from the new anti-Christian holocaust you seem to want to impose upon America.

[name withheld]

A little fact checking is needed here. Or sanity.

508.
October 25, 2013
Try looking down the barrel of a gun and tell me that you don't believe in God as you piss yourself.

If you don't like my religion in my Army then GET OUT and leave us Christians alone! If you bring down our military then who will save you from our enemies?

[name withheld]

515.

October 27, 2013

Have you considered trying NOT BEING SUCH A THIN SKINNED PUSSY who has to cry like a little bitch because you cant mentally separate yourself from concepts that you disagree with? have you read the declaration of independence and all of the references to "creator"? your oath does not advocate a particular religion which is what the separation of church and state is, "Congress shall make no law respecting an establishment of religion, or prohibiting the free exercise thereof " that includes your right NOT to practice. But lets all just bow down to pathetic fucks like yourself because your "offended" but its funny, i dont see where it the constitution that it says you have a right not to be offended by concepts or that concepts that you dont agree with must be hushed in order to accommodate your pathetic mind. actually, Im pretty sure the first amendment PROTECTS us from having idiots like yourself tell us

what we are allowed to say whether it pisses you off or not. Poor thing, how have you survived this long on a planet where so many people dont think like you forcing outside concepts into your tiny little mind???
[name withheld]

Well, I was going to make a comment here. But, no. Just, no.

568.
December 4, 2013
Dear MRFF,

Wow. How sad. You show you are not caving in to one religion by by caving in
to two other religions – Islam and Atheism. And then you say you are protecting
religious rights. Shameful.....
[name withheld]

2497.
December 13, 2013
Dear Mikey,
I am an athiest in the military, and I absolutely hate you, your organization, and what you are doing. Your actions are absolutely un-American

because you reject our Christian heritage which is undeniable. If I won the lottery, I would make it my purpose in life to destroy your organization in litigation, and drive you and all your American hating commies into poverty and then eject you from our country. It amazes me how you and the likes of you are so offended by the idea of Jesus Christ or anything Christian. As I said, I'm an athiest, but you guys take your cause so far that it disgusts me and other like minded people.

I hope you get a brain tumor and die for your Christmas present.

[name withheld]

This pronouncement of hate seems to fly in the face of "love thy neighbor." And, of course, the Christmas present statement isn't very nice. I must conclude that this person doesn't understand some of the basic tenets of Christianity.

650.
December 26, 2013
Dear MRFF,
You people need to shut up you dont like our nativity scenes our christmad lights tough shit.i personally would love to knock your teeth down your throats.stay out of our lives our religion's.

You are starting a war in which you people will get hurt badly.hope you choke and die you ignorant bastards.and those 18 military asswipes that complained better drop out .they will get theirs when we find out their names.go to hell bastards
[name withheld]

716.
April 24, 2014
Looks like weiny doesn't have a direct e-mail. Just want to let him know he is the biggest coward in America today. Why don't you stop hiding behind your titles and face the the 38 million people you hate so much. This country has no room for hate and as easy as it would be for to pack your trash and find another place to live you'd rather hide behind your titles and the constitution. Your a disgrace and your day of judgement will come like everyone else's. I'll continue to pray for you......
[name withheld]

So, "This country has no room for hate." And yet I read: "Pack your trash and find another place to live." And, "Your a disgrace and your day of judgement will come like everyone else's." Isn't that hate?

719.

April 25, 2014

Dear Mikey,

I am a retired Vet! I can honestly say your are or were an Officer in the Military because you have no clue what goes on in the Enlisted ranks. For over 20 years, I have come in contact with very few atheists and the ones who were atheists did not speak about being one. Those persons were generally not like and not trusted and the ones who wore their stance on their sleeve were just avoided and they did their time and got out. I can tell you never lead troops in the field or on the flight line, or commanded a squadron, or a ship, because leadership never influenced or gave personal opinion, or made religion mandatory.

I have an idea for you? Why don't you attack Islam or are you afraid? Islam is attacking the first amendment, the same one you blanket yourself with. Islam is where you should focusing your energy on and I garentee you that fight could pick up momentum. I am not sure who is disliked more, atheists or Islam, actually you guys are disliked more. I laugh at you because your are the one legged drunk guy getting his ass kicked by the little guys!

[name withheld]

724.
April 28, 2014
 Mr. Weinstein,
What you do to persecute the faithful of Christ in our military today is far worse than anything the Nazis were ever accused of doing to your jewish people. The same jewish people who rejected His grace and love. The same jewish people who crucified Him. Without mercy. (And one of their own.) As you Mr. Weinstein continue to do every day.
 Want to talk about a real holocaust day?
 You will suffer your own holocaust. Buring in hell forever. Semper Fi!
V/R
8 Active Duty Officers, USMC
Living For Jesus Christ in Act, Word and Deed
Spreading His Good News to All Marines We Can in the Corps

"Living For Christ in Act, Word and Deed."
Hmmmmmm?

Okay, I cannot lie. This letter amuses me. It is wholly ignorant, and I doubt the writer has ever met a Jewish person. He does, however, evangelize without hate or violence, and that's something, I guess. This writer is not shouting at me or wishing death and destruction upon my person. I cannot, however, figure out exactly whether I'm being complimented with "sophisticated Jew Princess" or being issued an insult (very mild in comparison, to be sure) with "dumb but beautiful shikees" (he means shiksa). I suspect after reading all of these letters, I have become terribly jaded. But, hey... Jeezus knows I'm human. You know, like Elvis.

27.
Sent to a MRFF supporter and volunteer:
what can I say~you found me out. Now I know
what they say about you Jew girls is absolutely true.
I suppose those Reform types just can't deal with
you smart, sophisticated Jew Princesses and that's
why they marry dumb, but beautiful shiksees~isn't
that what you call them. I'm one of those good ol
boys from the hill country of Tennessee. I only had
Jews on my maternal side~you know like Elvis,
and yes I really do believe you should take Jeezus
into your heart. In fact I have a little plastic Jeezus
mounted on my car dash! "I don't care if it rains
or freezes~cause I have my plastic Jeezus"! Won't
you take Jeezus as your Saviour~my precious little
Jew woman!

BONNIE AND THE FAMILY

After these letters were compiled and put into this chapter, I found myself continuously bypassing this section, telling myself I would deal with it later. When I finally had to address the selections, I started by skimming through the letters. It quickly dawned on me that I had never read many of these letters before, and it never ceases to amaze me how lucky I am to have married such a sweet and thoughtful man. I am very appreciative, both of my husband and the members of the Foundation, and want to thank them for diverting these letters and many of their ilk from my inbox when they first came in.

709.
April 10, 2014
From: Our Army Combat Unit's Daily Morning Bible Study Prayerful Soldiers

To: The MRFF's Evil Michael Weinstein

Message: Drop Dead. Preferably while you are driving into your driveway at home so you can hit as many family members as possible with your vehicle. Multiple dead Weinsteins for the price of one. Such a deal!

V/R
Proud Christians in the United States Army
Proud Americans in the Christian United States

***

"One-Minute Prayer: Let us pray. Almighty God, today we pray imprecatory prayers from Psalm 109 against the enemies of religious liberty, including Barry Lynn and Mikey Weinstein, who issued press releases this week attacking me personally. God, do not remain silent, for wicked men surround us and tell lies about us. We bless them, but they curse us. Therefore find them guilty, not me.Let their days be few, and replace them with Godly people. Plunder their fields, and seize their assets. Cut off their descendants, and remember their sins, in Jesus' name. Amen."

Klingenschmitt

***

1.
you f*****g piece of shit jew and your stinking jew woman and inbred jew childrun and jew-lover traiter daughterinlaw deserve to torture die

you filth jew liberil america hating jesus hating basterd Lord willing none of us will have to wait long america is too good for dirty jew scum of your family and your commie foundasion"

165.
March 24, 2011
Mickey:

It never ceases to amaze me to see otherwise mature and intelligent men allow their hatred to destroy their soul. However, your sin is much worse as you have been consumed by your hate and having allowed this to happen, you are now spewing your hatred and spreading it to all those around you. You are a despicable little elf who is eaten up with fear, resentment and false-pride.

I truly pray that your heart will quit or your brain will bleed-out or your liver will develop cancer. I hate you and what you are doing to our wonderful warriors and I pray God will remove you from this Earth sooner than later (really-I JUST said the prayer) so as to stop your hatred and the damage it has done and put an end to your insidious plans. I have prayed in the past for your Salvation, but having now seen that

He has turned you over to your ways, I am now praying for the death of you, your followers and co-conspirators.

319.
April 15, 2012
Dear Mikey,
you filhty stinking puny jewboy who fucks his whore diseased wife and breeds subhumain male and female jew- spawn as we see in your new jewshit book. in the pages never forget the faces of the jew family of Americas disgrace. about how you hateChristians and the Christian USA but love athiests and satan and muslem slimes. You crucified our Lord and laughed and made him suffer for your 20 pieces of silver jewboy mickey. and you nail Him to the Cross with your perverted constitution as the hammer in your evil jew paw. You hate the Word of God and the Bible and Xmas and chaplins and NRA and the Marines corps. You and your she-jew whore wife and jewshit retard children will burn in hell and you all don't care. How about we shove a nuke up your little laywer jewhole and nail you to the cross the very next time mickey fucker? Now let us pray for it everyday for it.
[name and e mail address withheld]

353.
June 19, 2012
Wepray Thee that our Lord and Savior bursts your aorta vein while you sleep and you wake up in death pain and drown choking in your own kike blood. Then, mickey jewboy you can think in your last moments before you burn in agony hell how you left your liberel black mfrr mark on Christ Jesus' America's army. pleasant dreams to you and your satan spawn family from hell.

7777.
July 1, 2012
hey kikey whinercrybabystein give it up already jewboy. your MFRR is just a bunches of queer lesbians and homos, kikes, sand nigger lovers and athiests, feminazis and hollywood spineless commies and of course totaly fake Christians. Who are not really true servints of Christ. You don't think we know this? your wife is made a pathitic cripple with no chance and your nasty spawn children are a disgrace to Christian America. And its Chrisitan army and military forces. which gave them and you there free education also. you jews just love that 'free' dont you kikey? Just like pigs to filth and garbage. its over for you all now. All of you are just fuel for the hellfire. You just don't know it yet. your family and chil-

dren and mfrr are just snakes and vipers. Jesus has
already sentenced you all to hell (Matthew 23:33).
There is no escape for you and your works of evil.
Our Lord and Savior knows your demon plans.
[name withheld]

379.
December 24, 2012
Christ was born and lives to conquer the World
with grace and His Word away from satan. The
U.S. of A was born to carry the Word of Jesus to
the fallen world at large. Our military is the sacred
instrument of Jesus to save the world from itself.
And etenity in Lake of Fire. You and your 'charity'
are the instruments of satan, mr. Mickey Wienstien. You use your jew lawyer clever traits to enslave
our soldiers away from the Only Truth ofChrist.
But you will fail of course. (2 Timothy 2:26) Only
the lake of Fire will be your award for all time. And
the inheritance of your evil wife and ugly children.
and all who serve you. You all will burn forver as
you serve the dark one. Merry Christmas to the
doomed fool mickey. Enemy of our Lord and Savior. your time to plunge draws close. And heaven
and earth will rejoice in your certain damnation.
'and you (wienstein) will be tormented day and
night forever and ever.' (Revelations 20:10)
[name withheld]

381.

February 7, 2013

Michael Weinstein of MFRR: You and your foundation are the largest threat to America. And it's historic and most important national Christian faith. My family and I and our church and pastor take happiness in knowing what Jesus will be doing to you and your family and followers of the darkness. As he will disembowel the antichrist and his evil legions, Christ will rip out your guts and the innards of your wife. And of your children and followers and worshipers of your dark path. Your spent entrails will pave the path for his Kingdom of Peace to come forever. This is your purpose. And what your inherit and deserve.

[name withheld]

8165.

March 22, 2013

Know how hated you are Micky kikeboy. Sandn***** and queer lover. Lord Jesus will take off your head. Like bin Ladens. and serve it to your stink trator wife. And coward children on silver platter. No escape for you. die.

393.

May 1, 2013

YOUR WHOLE DAMN FAMILY IS NOTHING MORE THAN WHITE TRASH. YOU MRS. WEINSTEIN ARE A WHORE AND YOUR HUSBAND HAS UNPROTECTED SEX WITH THE QUEER GOATS OF GAY MUSLIM MEN. I HOPE ALL YOUR FAMILY MEMBERS CONTRACT EXTREMELY PAINFUL RECTAL CANCER AND DIE !

have a nice day

400.

May 4, 2013

What a shame Hitler didn't wipe the seed of Weinstein off the face of the globe.

577.

December 8, 2013

is for your wife and children to have there heads explode with brain anyerisms. similtaniously. but not for you mickie jew. We want you to live with it for years and years to come. what the righteous hand of our Lord and Savior struck your little loved ones down with. and to think about it. its all because of you. What you and your father satan do. to keep the Only true Lord Christ

from our marines and flyers and soldiers. And from our nation. you think Jesus will not make you pay dearly? for your wickedness mickie jew? think again when you bury them all. if you love the US of A thank a Christian. semper fi And Merry Christmas.
[name withheld]

658.

January 2, 2014

May our Lord and savior sweep all of you away to you rightfull places burning in hell eternal. Starting with Mickey Weinstein. Who loves the fags muslems and jews more than he loves America and its people. May the new year bring Jesus wrath upon you all.
[name withheld]

659.

January 13, 2014

Mr. Wienstein,

Our Army Chaplain at our base bible study this morning asked us all to pray for your immortal soul. And the souls of your suffering wife and children. He said she has the MS. He has most of your alls' family pictures from the internet and FaceBook. We passed them around. And we prayed hard on them. And for the souls of all of the Lost to our Savior Jesus Christ at the military Religious freedom foundation.

721.
April 26, 2014
Mr. Mickey Whinestain a friend of a friend just told our bibly study group that you;re now a grand-parent. Did you ever ask yourself how will explain your ungodly satantic attack on the #1 faith of America-Christianity? To your poor grandchild when it grows up? You will be the biggest embar-rassment to that grandchild ever to be. You'll nev-er be able to live that down you evil one.
[name withheld]

728.
May 15, 2014
As Christ has cursed your devil children and their evil children for your sins of rebellion against Him. Mikey you are a ugly modern day Judas. John 18:1-40. A true demon. Luke 4: 31-37. And Christ Jesus will insure your eternal damnation for plot-ting with satan against His U.S. soldiers of faith. Matthew 7:19.
[name withheld]

730.

June 3, 2014

Bought your 'No Snowflake book'. Right after Fox news reported that Ayatollah Hussein Obama appointed (should we say 'annointed'?) you to persecute loving Christians in our U.S. armed forces. Burned that book right after reading it all. Spirit of Satan on every single page. Saw how you brought your fellow evildoers Joseph Wilson and Lawrence Wilkerson to your pentagon meeting. Our church is near a large Army base. Our church had a faith retreat this weekend. Many military families among us. You were the main topic. You are a very dangerous man to America, Michael Wienstein. You grow more dangerous every day. Especially to Jesus Christ. We have agreed that you are irredeemable. Now your forcing Christian paintings to be taken down on military bases. The pentagon is very afraid of you even. Of course that is Hussein Obama's plan. Because if they stand up to you you will sick our Muslim president on them. You have this demonic power of darkness in abundance. Saw the pictures of you and your family in the book. Too bad for you. And worse for them. We prayed at the retreat this weekend that they will surely burn for all time. In the unquechable fires of hell. For your willing sins. John 3:36.

Mark 9:43. We prayed that Wilson and Wilkerson will also burn in hell for your sins, Michael Weinstien. We prayed that you will be the last to burn. So that you may first experience the divine eternal suffering of your wife, children and Wilson and Wilkerson. Our Lord and Savior has promised us this. That He will make our prayers for you to witness those you love and care for suffer come true. It is already written. 1 John 5:14-15. Your time draws near. You think all is peaceful and secure for yourself and those you harbor. But there is no escape. 1 Thessaloninas 5:3. You will watch them all burn in chains forged by the Son of Man. And then you will burn, son of satan.

735.
July 18, 2014
We drove through you spic infested town of wet backs yesterday. Had the windows down. So we could smell the mixture of your kike stink and demon shame. on you and you're she kike bitch cripple wife. You try to bring your father satan to destroy our soldiers jewboy? No way. The Word shall defeat you. And lay you in ruins for eternity. But it is we who shall destroy you for the glory of Christ. You are death and will be destroyed by The Lamb. 1 Corinthians 15:26

3499.

May 20, 2014

Mr. Mikey Weinstein you are the Number One Enemy of America. You don't deserve American citizenship. You deserve no safety nor sanctuary. You should be hunted down like an animal with rabies. You are our country's foremost enemy. Along with your Jesus-hating organization MRFF. You take no Christian prisoners Mr. Weinstein? Why should you receive any mercy?

It makes sense that you have other American traitors as fellow travelers of deceit. Joseph Wilson is such a traitor. Mike Farrell is also such a traitor. Lawrence Wilkerson is a snake who betrays even his own Republicans. Edward Asner is a red godless communist like you are.

But you are the slimebag responsible for it all. Your evil grows substantial. The father of lies is your benefactor. Lucifer leads you in your rebellion against Christ in our military.

All of us with a clean heart and soul for the Son of Man see this. His Grace reveals your treachery. We pray to the Son that your days be few and your suffering be unbearable.

That you live only so long as to see your children and wife despoiled. Ravaged and ruined before your eyes.

We pray to Him that your tears be unending.
Let your tears be of acid so as to burn your jew face
of darkness threw to the bone.
[name withheld]

371.
September 25, 2012
pray the Psalm 109 to our Lord and Savior Christ
Jesus to mightily shorten the days of life for the evil
children and the wicked wife of the demon mickey wienstien. Who worships mulsims and homos,
abortions and satan and money. But pray that Jesus keeps the demon mickey living for many years.
so that he brutaly suffers the loss of his brood and
spawn all the days of his life. as he makes the saved
children of the Lord Jesus suffer. By taking Christianity and The Word away from our army and our
nation of Christians. Pray the Psalm 109.
[name withheld]

The Psalms
109

A Cry for Vengeance
To the chief Musician, A Psalm of David.

1 Hold not thy peace, O God of my praise;

2 for the mouth of the wicked and the mouth of the deceitful are opened against me: they have spoken against me with a lying tongue.

3 They compassed me about also with words of hatred; and fought against me without a cause.

4 For my love they are my adversaries: but I give myself unto prayer.

5 And they have rewarded me evil for good, and hatred for my love.

6 Set thou a wicked man over him: and let Satan stand at his right hand.

7 When he shall be judged, let him be condemned: and let his prayer become sin.

8 Let his days be few; and let another take his office. Acts 1.20

9 Let his children be fatherless, and his wife a widow.

10 Let his children be continually vagabonds, and beg: let them seek their bread also out of their desolate places.

11 Let the extortioner catch all that he hath; and let the strangers spoil his labor.

12 Let there be none to extend mercy unto him: neither let there be any to favor his fatherless children.

13 Let his posterity be cut off; and in the generation following let their name be blotted out.

14 Let the iniquity of his fathers be remembered with the LORD; and let not the sin of his mother be blotted out.

15 Let them be before the LORD continually, that he may cut off the memory of them from the earth.

16 Because that he remembered not to show mercy, but persecuted the poor and needy man, that he might even slay the broken in heart.

17 As he loved cursing, so let it come unto him: as he delighted not in blessing, so let it be far from him.

18 As he clothed himself with cursing like as with his garment, so let it come into his bowels like water, and like oil into his bones.

19 Let it be unto him as the garment which cov-ereth him, and for a girdle wherewith he is girded continually.

20 Let this be the reward of mine adversaries from the LORD, and of them that speak evil against my soul.

21 But do thou for me, O GOD the Lord, for thy name's sake: because thy mercy is good, deliver thou me.

22 For I am poor and needy, and my heart is wounded within me.

23 I am gone like the shadow when it declineth: I am tossed up and down as the locust.

24 My knees are weak through fasting; and my flesh faileth of fatness.

25 I became also a reproach unto them: when they looked upon me they shook their heads. Mt. 27.39 · Mk. 15.29

26 Help me, O LORD my God: O save me according to thy mercy:

27 that they may know that this is thy hand; that thou, LORD, hast done it.

28 Let them curse, but bless thou: when they arise, let them be ashamed; but let thy servant rejoice.

29 Let mine adversaries be clothed with shame; and let them cover themselves with their own confusion, as with a mantle.

30 I will greatly praise the LORD with my mouth; yea, I will praise him among the multitude.

31 For he shall stand at the right hand of the poor, to save him from those that condemn his soul.

THE REAl CONStItUtIoN

We the Fundamentalist Evangelical Christian People of the United States, in Order to form a more perfect Dominion, establish world order and insure domestic Christianity for the

*I*t is good to be able to carry on discussions with people. We do answer every single letter that comes in. In many cases, a healthy email exchange ensues. However, I have thought to myself on many occasions, especially after reading the letters in this section, *Are people being dumb on purpose?* Or, *Did they just sleep through every single class in school? Are they re-writing history to comfort themselves?* Or, *Do they really think they have one iota of knowledge of the subject to which they speak?*

104.
April 30, 2010
Mr Wienstien
Let's not only eliminate the National Day of Prayer, let us also free ourselves from any and all influences of religion.
That would mean eliminating the following from our laws
1 all laws prohibiting theft of any kind
2 all laws prohibiting murder
3 all laws prohibiting false testimony
4 all marital laws
The above listed items have their foundation based in religion. So, based on your desire and that theory, because those laws on the books are

unconstitutional, I am free to steal your car, take your life, lie to the authorities about it, and sleep with your wife.

Just an english lesson to you on the meaning of the words of and from

Entry Word: of

Function: preposition

Meaning: 1 earlier than <it's ten minutes of two right now> — see before 1

2 having to do with <the librarian read stories of kings and princesses to the group>

Main Entry: from

Pronunciation: \⬚frⅢm, Ⅲfräm also fⅢm\

Function: preposition

Etymology: Middle English, from Old English from, fram; akin to Old High German fram, adverb, forth, away, Old English faran to go — more at fare

Date: before 12th century

1 a —used as a function word to indicate a starting point of a physical movement or a starting point in measuring or reckoning or in a statement of limits <came here from the city> <a week from today> <cost from $5 to $10> b —used as a function word to indicate the starting or focal point of an activity <called me from a pay phone> <ran a business from her home>

2 —used as a function word to indicate physical separation or an act or condition of removal, abstention, exclusion, release, subtraction, or differentiation <protection from the sun> <relief from anxiety>

3 —used as a function word to indicate the source, cause, agent, or basis <we conclude from this> <a call from my lawyer> <inherited a love of music from his father> <worked hard from necessity>

The 1st amendment guarantees me freedom OF religion not freedom FROM religion. In other words I can talk, pray and worship publicly to the god of my choice without government intervention. Both you and Judge Crabb must have been snorting something behind the bleachers during American History class to miss that very important lesson. Just to piss the both of you off I am going to encourage our troops to pray on May 6th on base. I DARE you to stop me

What is really sad is that this person most likely took a lot of time to write that.

181.
August 3, 2011
Dear MRFF:

Separation of church and state is not possible. Without religion, we have no morals or ethics. The government is made up of "we the people". Last time I checked, most people practice religion. Hard to separate religion and belief from people.

Groups like yours will ruin our country.
[name withheld]

580.
December 10, 2013
You guys are clearly a communist, atheistic organization that knows nothing about religious freedom. Christmas is about Jesus. If people don't want to look at the nativity scene, they can look the other way. The Constitution quote that you quote on your web site means that the Government will not establish a State run church that exercises control over the other churches, like what the Church of England did. That's it, nothing else. The constitution talks about freedom of religion, not freedom from religion. Any attempt to restrict religion is un-constitutional. Bottom line: The

Government is never, ever, to interfere in the affairs of the church. The church is free to run rampant in society without any restrictions, regardless of what the courts say. The constitution trumps all Air Force regulations that people try to hide behind. Your organization needs to promote religious freedom, not restrict it.
[name withheld]

"The church is free to run rampant in society without any restrictions, regardless of what the courts say." No. No, it's not. It's really easy to dismiss these people as completely nuts and move on, but the sheer amount of them out there is truly disturbing.

4176.
December 11, 2013
You are violating my rights
[name withheld]

85.
Dear MRFF,

I just watched a video with your founder proselytizing on the constitutionality of religion in america specifically the military. I have to say, I am very disappointed that an organization like yours that advocates religious freedom would then argue why those religious freedoms should be taken away based on your very weak interpretation of our Constitution. I would suggest and encourage your founder and your staff to do your homework before espousing your belief. One can certainly have an opinion, just make sure you know what your talking about before you give it.

There is no such thing as "separation of church and state". Why your founder continues to use this phrase is suspect. This phrase was used as a metaphor in a letter from Thomas Jefferson to the Danberry Baptists concerning the the thanksgiving holiday. NOWHERE in the Constitution does it suggest or imply that the state should be separated from the church. Regarding religion, the Constitution says is:
Amendment 1 - Freedom of Religion, Press, Expression. Ratified 12/15/1791.
Congress shall make no law respecting an establishment of religion, or prohibiting the free exercise thereof; The state cannot "establish" an institution of religion for the people. Pretty clear to me prohibiting the free exercise thereof; The state CANNOT prevent a person from exercising his right to express his belief.

It does NOT say unless you are a "Christian" or "in the military"

I would also like to point out that the officers and enlisted men that claim to be "christians" and harassing their subordinates, are a far cry from what a christian is supposed to be. I would submit that they show evidence that they are not "christian" at all.

The government is supposed to protect the peoples inalienable rights that were granted to us by God. The founders knew this and was part of the Declaration of Independence.

705.
March 26, 2014
Dear Mikey,

You are a sham, a farce, a fraud and an evil. You speak out of a severe lack of understanding of life itself. The separation of church and state is to PROTECT the church from the state, and I believe you know this. How you, and many others of your kind, have perverted it, is beyond obvious.
[name withheld]

...IN THE END

My husband receives threats on a daily basis. They come in through his various phones, snail mail, and his email. They often increase significantly right before a business trip. He's asked to give speeches and participate in seminars all over the nation. As the threats continue to pour in and are more specific in nature, security has become much more of an issue. It's imperative that security precautions are taken while we are traveling as a family, and everywhere Mikey speaks. We both have had to become so much more aware of our surroundings and the people around us. Many of the letters in this book come from paper tigers, people who are emboldened by the security and anonymity of the internet. These paper tigers create fake email addresses and fake names. On rare occasions, there have been people who have signed their real name with a real email address. I have to give credit to those people, at least they are willing to attach their name to what they have written. I wonder though, would these same people actually say this to us in normal conversation if we were face to face? My guess is…no.

37.
Weinstein should be drawn and quartered. I know some Marines who could do the job.

242.
November 8, 2011
Dear Military Religious Freedom Foundation,

YES, JESUS EVEN LOVES sorry ones like you. IT IS A SHAME THAT IT WILL BE TOO LATE FOR YOU, WHEN YOU FIND OUT, BECAUSE YOU WILL BE BURNING IN HELL WITH madelyn ohara & son.
LONG LIVE THE PRO-CHRISTIAN AND PRO-ISRAEL MOVEMENTS!!!

ISLAM SUX & SO DO YOU

354.
June 21, 2012
....coming soon to a bookstore near you is 'No Weinstein Left Alive in a Avalanche'.
[name and e mail withheld]

376.

November 7, 2012

the nigger won and you kikes and you raghead islams and the homos you worship can celebrate in
the damnation our Lord and savior will bring on
your evil heads. Jesus will not be denied and the
USA military will be Christs right arm. The End
is coming and you and MFRR will be destroyed
by the breath of Jesus mouth, demon mickey. (2
thessalonians 2:8).

387.

April 20, 2013

My husband is a proud USMC sniper. We and
our children and all the real marines in our unit
are proud Christians. We all walk our life in the
Lord's Word. This means that it is our number
one job to bring the lost to the Word and Grace of
our Savior. By all the means necessary. If we fail to
do so all who do not find Christ will burn in the
darkness of hell. Mr. Mikey Wienstien has dedicated his earthly life to satan. To trying to stop marines and soldiers and the American forces from
bringing the fallen world to Christ. And most of
the world is fallen. Christ is the one and only way.
This makes Mikey the number one enemy of the
Savior. Mikey on tv. Mikey on the radio. Mikey

in the magazines and newspapers and Mikey all over the internet. Mikey won't stop defying Christ and persecuting his followers in the service. But Mikey's earthly life will end one day soon we pray. It is then he will pay. It's then we will sing and smile. Our prayer circle on base is large and effective. Our prayer circle prayer is a dream of a world with no Mikey Wienstein in it. The dream we share is of Mikey in hell on fire and screaming. And screaming and screaming and screaming. As the flames bake him. For all eternity as our Lord has proclaimed. And noone can hear him. Noone can help him. Watch Mikey sceam in our dream. Here Mikey scream in our dream. Forever in hell with his friends the homos, the muslems the communists, the leftists. And the gun haters and the abortion lovers. Christ makes all things new again. Christ answers the prayers of his faithful. and noone is more faithful to Christ than the USMC. Burn, burn Mikey burn. Halleluya
[name withheld]

2001.
April 30, 2013
Dear Mikey,
I am amazed, I look at your site and if we disagree with you its labeled hate mail!

Actually, it is quite the contrary. If people disagree with us, and we can engage them in discourse, we do communicate. And often quite effectively.

Wow, you tell a chaplain he can't witness to someone who could face God!

I believe this writer is trying to say that he is upset because we are suggesting chaplains stay within the legal boundaries of their job and not prey on people who are in no position to stand up for themselves.

You call it spiritual rape? I am a retired military and I would have laughed in your face at what you are suggesting.

Members of the United States Military have sworn to protect and defend the Constitution. No laughing allowed.

I applaud our chaplains who are with us in combat.

As do we.

You are a wolf in Sheep's clothing...

More like a wolf in wolf's clothing. We never appear to be anything other than what we are.

...you claim republican, liar!

I have known my husband quite a few years now and I can honestly say, beyond a shadow of a doubt, he is not a liar.

Go ahead and add this to your "hate" mail. Because I will fight what your trying to do to the military who have the very real possibility to put off this mortal coil and they need to have the peace that Christ gives.

This writer is suggesting that ALL members of the military need to have "the peace that Christ gives," and...therein lies the problem.

If you don't see that we'll who's the hater now?

That's just it. We do see the issue, as do many. Thus the reason for our "interference." We do not hate. We simply give back what we receive. Sometimes that is the only way to get through to people.

I pray You meet Jesus before its too late.

Thank you for the thought.

But I promise this I will oppose your plans and peacefully fight you with millions of others who disagree with you and you don't have the guts to discuss with you just label it hate, ironic when it's love.
[name withheld]

Fortunately, we live in a nation that allows its citizens to discuss issues both publicly and privately. We don't have to agree with each other, either. I am sorry that people think that in order to discuss anything with the Foundation they need to steel themselves in some way. I know it takes some intestinal fortitude to be able to voice your opinion and stand up for your ideas in any way, no matter how correct or incorrect they may be, but we hope to create an open dialogue through the work of MRFF, a dialogue that can open minds and help people rethink their preconceived notions.

We are acutely aware that when most people evangelize to others, they do it from a good place in their heart. This writer would call it

"love." But, this "love," when delivered in the US Military, MUST be in accordance with the US Constitution, its federal, and state case law, and all military directives, instructions, and regulations. Unfortunately, in so many cases, it is not, and that's where we come in.

628.
December 15, 2013
I hope they hunt you
[name withheld]

664.
February 5, 2014
Michael Weinstein,
You, sir, and your repulsive family are the most disgraceful plague ever to be visited upon our beloved Air Force Academy. What you and your so-called "Military Freedom FROM Religious Foundation" have done to destroy the Academy's good name can only be described as evil incarnate. You are so despised in the Academy graduate community. How does that make you feel?
And no little forgetable speech by the Academy Dean will ever change what you are. You are an isolated outcast forever among your fellow graduates..
Know how much you are hated Michael Wein-

stein. Know how much your fellow USAFA graduates will rejoice when you eventually croak. You
will go straight to hell for your deliberate crimes
of rebellion against America, its special Christian
heritage of anointment and our Lord and Savior
Jesus Christ.

We can't wait to piss on your grave, Weinstein.
Fast, Neat, Average, Friendly, Dead, Dead.

signed,
many graduates of the United States Air Force
Academy
Proud to be Christians
Proud to be Americans

734.
June 26, 2014
Weinstein controls Obama's military. Force's the
soldiers of Christ to pray to evil weinstein. Now
that we all know who and what he is the only question is what will we do to stop him dead in his
tracks?

From: sgtusa@forttilvery.com
Subject: Your grave will be a public toilet
Date: August 28, 2014 at 9:07:50 AM MDT

To: Mikey Weinstein

When you croak weinstein you best have a un-marked grave? Know alot of good folks who will love to piss and take a dump on it if not. The MRFF is just like ISIS but even worse. You love the muslims better than your own American Christians? We all know why. Because you hide behind the constitution? play hide and seek with The Truth of Christ's Gospel. You pretend to help the troops. But you only want to keep The Good News from us and our families. Yes Jesus was a Jew. But not the deceiver kind you are. Sooner your in hell the sooner His Will Be Done. Give it up weinstein and surrender to His Word. Or else you burn. Very disrespectfully,, 7 US Army Noncoms and our wifes and children

Many letters presented in this book aren't try-ing to give an argument or take a stand in dis-cussing how or why the detractors feel a certain way. They simply hate. And they hate well. It's just disturbing to see it. I know Mikey shrugs them off, but I, for one, am tired of living with such hate—hate that seeps into every aspect of our lives. Our lives have become the Foundation and it's no doubt consumed us. I long for the trajectory that our life was on before we became

pissed-off parents and stepped in to help. I'm not sorry that we started the Foundation, but it will be nice to continually gain more ground and eventually achieve some kind of normalcy with our fight. All of this may be more of a journey than a destination, and our hope is with the future: that things will get better for everyone concerned.

From: trewblu@frgorra.com
Subject: Fuck you weinstien
Date: September 11, 2014 at 2:42:05 PM MDT
To: Information Weinstein <mikey@militaryreligiousfreedom.org>

Air Force is right to put God in the oath. mikey weinstien is wrong to even still be breething. Air force should save a bomb from dropping on ISIS and drop it on mikey.

December 19, 2011
Dear MRFF,

Be Afraid, be very afraid – – – The Christians are coming!!!
[name withheld]

I am trying not to play Devil's advocate here, pun intended, but I simply have to ask each and every one of the people that write into the Foundation with such hate on behalf of their benevolent Lord:

WWJW...What Would Jesus Write?

ACHIEVEMENTS

Military Religious Freedom Foundation
Select List & Chronology of Achievements

August 2007
MRFF Exposes Distribution of Fundamentalist Christian Propaganda to Deployed US Troops

MRFF was first to uncover unconstitutional distribution of sectarian and bigoted *Left Behind* videogame to active-duty troops serving in Iraq: The game features a postapocalyptic storyline where "Soldiers for Christ" must convert "Secularists," Jews, Muslims, and others. The evangelical extremist group Operation Straight Up, which provided the games, openly advocates the United States military unleashing "multiple crusades" to "sweep through" the Arab and Muslim world.

August 2007
MRFF Exposes Christian Embassy's Unprecedented Access to the DoD Hierarchy

Department of Defense (DoD) Inspector General's report, instigated by MRFF, finds misconduct by uniformed Pentagon Generals participating in "Christian Embassy" promo video filmed inside the Pentagon.

October 2008
MRFF Garners Endorsement of Major Christian Organization

The California Council of Churches IMPACT (CCCI), one of the country's largest Christian organizations, representing twenty-one mainstream and progressive Protestant denominations, 5,500 congregations, and millions of congregants formally announces its endorsement of MRFF.

October 2009
MRFF Receives Nobel Peace Prize Nomination

The Military Religious Freedom Foundation is officially nominated for the 2010 Nobel Peace Prize. The nominator, who wishes to remain anonymous, happens to be the only Christian in the upper chamber of his country's national parliament. That country is an ally of the United States. Shortly thereafter, another anonymous Qualified Nominator submits a second official nomination for MRFF for the same.

January 2010
MRFF Uncovers Shipment of "Jesus Rifles" to US and Allied Troops Deployed to the Middle East

On ABC's flagship news program *Nightline*, MRFF and Mikey Weinstein exposed various biblical references engraved on Trijicon brand rifle scopes used by the United States military in Iraq and Afghanistan. The breaking story exploded across international news outlets. Shortly after the "Jesus Rifles" story broke, the manufacturer gave in to media pressure, ceased inscribing new scopes for the military, and distributed inscription-removal kits to the DoD for use on weapons already deployed worldwide.

April 2010
MRFF Action Blocks Islamophic Preacher's Participation in National Day of Prayer Event

MRFF successfully demands the cancellation of Islamophobic Evangelical Preacher Franklin Graham's scheduled participation in the Pentagon's National Day of Prayer event, thereby severing the affiliation between the Pentagon event and Shirley Dobson's (wife of Focus on the Family founder, James Dobson) exclusively Christian National Day of Prayer Task Force so as to make this event inclusive of all religions.

MRFF Research Director Contributes Chapter to Official U.S. Air Force Publication

Also in April, the book *Attitudes Aren't Free: Thinking Deeply about Diversity in the US Armed Forc-*

es, published by Air University at Maxwell Air Force Base, is widely distributed throughout the command structure of the United States military. The book includes a chapter written by MRFF Senior Research Director Chris Rodda and provides a comprehensive overview along with numerous specific examples of the various issues that MRFF is currently dealing with and has dealt with in the past.

June 2010
MRFF Receives Significant Endorsement from Religious Alliance

MRFF challenged the Evans Army Community Hospital emblem's depiction of a Crusader cross. Colorado Interfaith Alliance officially supported and endorsed MRFF's efforts.

August 2010
MRFF Exposes Forced Attendance at Christian Proselytizing Concerts

MRFF breaks the story of soldiers punished for refusing to attend a Christian concert at Ft. Eustis. MRFF's spotlight on the issue of military-endorsed Christian concerts led to significant criticism of the Billy Graham Association's "Rock the Fort" Christian concert at Ft. Bragg the following month. Exorbitant costs to the military/DoD in taxpayer dollars used to pay for the concerts also exposed.

September 2010
MRFF Heralded as "Constitutional Conscience of the Military"

MRFF and Mikey are included as major subjects in *The New York Times* bestselling author Jeff Sharlet's groundbreaking book, *C Street: The Fundamentalist Threat to American Democracy* published by Little, Brown and Company in which they are referred to as the "constitutional conscience of the military."

October 2010
MRFF Receives National and International Recognition

MRFF is officially nominated for the 2011 Nobel Peace Prize, making this the second consecutive year MRFF is honored with such recognition. Mikey Weinstein receives the 2010 Anne Froehlich Political Courage Award from the Pacific Palisades Democratic Club for his work with the Foundation.

November 2010
MRFF Forces Release of USAFA Survey

After MRFF's relentless pressure on the US Air Force Academy (USAFA), Superintendent Lt. Gen. Gould releases the data behind the biannual Academy Climate Survey. The survey reveals that 41% of non-Christian cadets and 19% of all cadets were subjected to unwanted proselytizing. Additionally, religious liberty watchdog Americans United for Separation of Church and State announces that Mikey Weinstein will be named "Person of the Year" at a November 2011 ceremony in Washington, DC. "We've never named a 'Person of the Year' before, but I can't think of anyone more deserving than Mikey Weinstein," stated Americans United executive director Rev. Barry W. Lynn.

Throughout 2010
MRFF Establishes Significant Impact on the Training of US Military Leaders

Mikey Weinstein speaks to students at a number of the US military's educational institutions including the USAFA's National Character and Leadership Symposium, the Air Force JAG School, and the Air Command and Staff College. This direct contact with the future leaders of America's military has been vitally important to MRFF's continuing mission of fostering a climate of absolute religious freedom and acceptance throughout our armed forces.

January 2011
MRFF Sheds Light On and Demands Correction to "Spiritual Fitness" Evaluation of Military Personnel

MRFF demands that the US Army cease and desist its blatantly unconstitutional policy of administering the "spiritual fitness" component—in fact, a religious test which the Constitution explicitly bars—as part of their "Soldier Fitness Tracker," an assessment of their combat readiness and abilities.

March 8, 2011
MRFF Opposes Superiors Demanding Participation in Religious Events

US Army releases an investigation on March 8, 2011, pursuant to MRFF demands: Soldiers reported to MRFF that they were disciplined after choosing not to attend evangelical Christian "Commanding Generals" Spiritual Fitness concert at Ft. Eustis. MRFF continues to disagree with the investigation's attempt to place the blame on a lower-ranking soldier.

March 24, 2011
Religious Climate Review Team Begins Evaluation at USAFA

Due to pressure from MRFF, a Religious Climate Review Team, led by General Patrick K. Gamble, USAF (ret.), begins seeking comments from USAFA cadets and faculty about impressions of and experiences with the religious climate at the Air Force Academy. This review is not an investigation or compliance inspection, but rather an independent look—sadly done with the narrowest of

views through cover-up blinders—at at the overall
religious climate at USAFA.

March 29, 2011
MRFF Invited to Provide Testimony to the US Senate

On March 29, 2011, MRFF provides extensive
written testimony to a US Senate hearing on "Protecting the Civil Rights of American Muslims."
The hearing is held before the Senate Committee
on the Judiciary, Subcommittee on the Constitution, Civil Rights and Human Rights, and is the
first ever Congressional hearing on the civil rights
of American Muslims.

April 15, 2011
MRFF Exposes Flawed Process and Illegitimacy of Gamble Report on USAFA Climate Study

The findings released on April 15, 2011 by the
Religious Climate Review Team find no evidence
at any level that anyone fears for their physical safety based upon their religious beliefs or nonbelief.
MRFF believes that these findings are radically
different from the 2010 Climate Survey based on
a fatally flawed review process. As one Academy
faculty member (and MRFF client) writes after
reading Gamble's report, which includes a section
on the investigation's methodology: "You don't do

proper research with a self-selected sample—unless, of course, you are fishing for the answers you already want... Frankly, General Gamble, I expected better. This Gamble Report would be laughed out of committee even as a master's degree proposal. It doesn't even make a good term paper." MRFF released a response that the report by Gamble's Team was completely inadequate and a shallow attempt to whitewash the actual situation on the ground at the USAFA.

May 13, 2011
ABC News Reports on MRFF's Muslim Clients Persecuted for Religious Beliefs

"[The United States is] at war with Islam and you are a Muslim." These shocking and inflammatory words were not uttered by a radical Al Qaeda ideologue such as Ayman al-Zawahiri but by an officer of the US Army Criminal Investigation Division, addressing honorable men eager to serve their adopted homeland. These unfounded accusations and the subsequent witch hunt were prominently featured by Pat Robertson's Christian Broadcasting Network, an international television network known for its opposition to America's foundational principles of religious freedom and the separation of church and state. After having endured forty-five days of detention, the Muslim soldiers are abruptly released without explanation (unsurprisingly, CBN fails to report on the unproven nature of the allegations once the soldiers are released). However, the charges have already stuck: unable to find a job, pass background checks, or even win the scantest form of redress from the Army, Khalid Lyaacoubi and Yassine Bahammou reach out to MRFF.

Springing into action immediately, MRFF mobilizes all resources at its disposal to get this horrific experience into the national and international spotlight so that Khalid and Yassine's ordeal would be known. Due to MRFF's unflagging persistence, the resulting investigations by both *The New York Times* and ABC News' flagship program *Nightline* reveal that the forty-five day detention is the tip of the iceberg, with disruptive effects resulting from this massive human rights violation continuing to erect huge barriers in the lives of these aspiring citizen-patriots whose only goal is to serve the United States of America.

July 5, 2011
MRFF Compels Investigation into Bibles Imprinted with Official Service Seals

Airman/Soldier Bibles (with the respective official service seal on the cover) are found for sale at the [USAF installation name withheld] Air Force Base BX. These insignias represent governmental endorsement. Placed on bibles, they represent un-Constitutional governmental endorsement of religion. In a few short hours, after initial contact at the request of a MRFF client, a very senior general officer contacts the client regarding this issue and promises to look into it. At that point, he promises to do whatever he can to get these Bibles removed from the shelves of the BX. A few days later, the MRFF client receives a follow-up call from the general saying the issue has been elevated to the DoD General Counsel's Office to investigate why the official service seals of the USAF, US Army, Navy, and Marines Corps are on these Bibles in the first place. MRFF's client, an active duty Air Force Judge Advocate, expresses doubt that this outcome would have been achieved without MRFF's involvement.

July 7, 2011
MRFF Takes Vocal Stand in Support of Religious Freedom Policies at Houston VA Cemetery

MRFF and VCF send a joint letter to Erik Shinseki, Secretary of the Department of Veterans affairs, regarding the shocking level of misinformation and legal ignorance of the Liberty Institute and Tea Party extremists. After reviewing VA's policies, MRFF and VCF agrees with and supports the expression (or lack) of religious preferences by families. MRFF and VCF also forcefully denounces the transparent and crass opportunism of the Liberty Institute and Tea Party to create a controversy where none had previously existed. Those organizations are fostering fear with their baseless allegations of religious censorship, when, in fact, there is an abundance of religious freedom. MRFF and VCS object to the hidden partisan agenda using VA facilities to proselytize on hallowed grounds before, during, and after funeral services for our honorable veterans and their loving family members. MRFF and VCS urge the VA to continue publicizing the agency's policy of "respecting every veteran and their family's right to a burial service that honors their faith tradition," especially when no religion or religious preference is chosen by the deceased and his or her family.

July 14, 2011
CNN's *Anderson Cooper 360°* Airs Report on Taxpayer-Funded Fake "Ex-Terrorist" Previously Exposed by MRFF in 2008

MRFF first becomes aware of Walid Shoebat, Zachariah Anani, and Kamal Saleem back in early 2008, when they were invited to speak at the USA-

FA's 50th Annual Academy Assembly on the topic "Dismantling Terrorism: Developing Actionable Solutions for Today's Plague of Violence," for a fee of $13,000. After demands by MRFF for equal time to counter the anti-Muslim screed of Shoebat and his fellow self-proclaimed ex-terrorists-turned-evangelical Christians, the Air Force Academy eventually allows MRFF founder and president Mikey Weinstein (himself an Academy graduate), MRFF Advisory Board member and Islam expert Reza Aslan, and MRFF Board member and former Ambassador Joe Wilson to speak to (i.e. deprogram) the cadets.

July 27, 2011
MRFF Aids Authorities Regarding AWOL Soldier Charged in Ft. Hood Bomb Plot

Jason Naser Abdo originally contacts MRFF in late 2010. MRFF "never felt good about him," thus refuses to represent Abdo in his discharge attempt as a conscientious objector. Information provided by MRFF clients aids authorities in Adbo's arrest.

July 29, 2011
MRFF Discredits Then Compels Corrective Action Regarding "Jesus Nukes"

Based on the fallout from a MRFF client's FOIA request exposing the use of Christian "Just War" theology within the mandatory training for missileers, the Nuclear Ethics and Nuclear Warfare training program "has been taken out of the curriculum and is being reviewed," according to David Smith, chief of public affairs of Air Education and Training Command at Randolph Air Force Base in Texas. Subsequent to this action, on August 14, 2011, the *Air Force Times* reports that the Air Force is reviewing all training materials related to ethics, core values, and character development after more exclusively Christian-themed course work surfaced.

August 4, 2011
Fort Bragg Limits—then Restores—Promised Support for "Rock Beyond Belief" Concert/Festival

In response to the aforementioned exclusively evangelical Christian concerts and, in particular, "Rock the Fort" event, nonbelieving soldiers are supported by MRFF in their request for fair treatment, vis-a-vis their own "Rock Beyond Belief" event. A spokesman for Fort Bragg announces in early August 2011 that: "Our logistical support will be the same as what we did for Rock the Fort," meaning Bragg will provide the venue, security, and basic utilities. The event is then scheduled to take place on March 31, 2012, on the main parade field at Fort Bragg (also the venue for the Billy

Graham Evangelistic Association's fundamentalist Christian "Rock the Fort" concert which is officially endorsed and promoted by Fort Bragg).

August 9, 2011
MRFF Exposes Use of Christian Messaging Extending to US Air Force ROTC Program

An Air Force Instructor and MRFF client provides MRFF with training slides used in a lesson designed to teach the Air Force's core values to ROTC cadets. Slides focusing exclusively on Christian beliefs (such as the Ten Commandments, the Sermon on the Mount, and the Golden Rule) are used as examples of ethical values. Slides go on to explain what each of them are (for example, listing seven of the Ten Commandments).

August 19, 2011
MRFF Exposes DoD Contracts Regarding Religious Proselytizing to Military Members and Families

In 2010, MRFF begins an investigation into just how much money the DoD spends promoting religion to military personnel and their families. The initial report by Chris Rodda, MRFF Senior Research Director, was released on August 19, 2011, and was prominently featured on the front page of *The Huffington Post*.

September 1, 2011
MRFF Instrumental in Development and Implementation of US. Air Force Instruction 1-1, Section 2.11 Regarding Religious Neutrality

On September 1, 2011, General Norton Schwartz, United States Air Force Chief of Staff, issues a directive on "Maintaining Government Neutrality Regarding Religion." Distribution of this directive at USAFA only occurrs after MRFF's placement of a copy of that directive on a billboard near the main entrance to the USAFA..

October 19, 2011
MRFF Defends US Army Soldier's Decision to Ignore Forced Prayer

A soldier calls MRFF after taking part in a rehearsal for a graduation ceremony where officials order soldiers to bow their heads and clasp their hands during the chaplain's benediction. As an atheist, the soldier refused to do so. "I immediately pointed out that not only is a prayer at a public ceremony unconstitutional, but to force someone to give the illusion of religion when the individual does not believe in any religion is blatantly wrong and very illegal," the soldier states in an e-mail to the Foundation. After quick intervention by Mikey Weinstein, Fort Jackson officials decide it is okay for the soldier to stand at attention.

November 1, 2011
MRFF & UNLV Secular Student Alliance Confront Fred Phelps & Westboro Baptist Church

On Tuesday, November 1st, 2011, the Secular Student Alliance at the University of Nevada, Las Vegas joins forces with MRFF to counter the presence of the Westboro Baptist Church at UNLV. The "Church," keeping in step with its characteristically aimless campaign of all-around religious hatred, is protesting the University itself, claiming that it "offers courses in rebellion against God" and "advanced degrees in Proud Sin and Perversion." The UNLV Secular Student Alliance uses the event to raise money for MRFF and its mission.

November 3, 2011
MRFF Forces Immediate Corrective Actions Pertaining to Missionary Program Backed By Fundamentalist Franklin Graham at the USAFA

MRFF's demands for compliance with General Schwartz's directive of September 1, 2011 leads to USAFA's command quickly moving sponsorship and oversight of Franklin Graham's Operation Christmas Child program at USAFA to the Chaplain Corps, where it belongs.

November 7, 2011
MRFF's Mikey Weinstein named AU Person of the Year 2011

Americans United for Separation of Church and State awarded Mikey Weinstein its inaugural Person of the Year award in Washington, DC on November 7, 2011. "We've never named a 'Person of the Year' before, but I can't think of anyone more deserving than Mikey Weinstein," stated Americans United executive director Rev. Barry W. Lynn.

November 11, 2011
MRFF Nominated for the 2012 Nobel Peace Prize

The Military Religious Freedom Foundation, the only nonprofit organization that is solely dedicated to working tirelessly to stop unconstitutional religious discrimination and oppression in the United States armed forces, is nominated for the 2012 Nobel Peace Prize, marking the third consecutive year that MRFF has received a nomination for this prestigious honor. While the Nobel committee does not officially release the names of nominees for fifty years, the letter nominating the MRFF is authorized for release by the Foundation, though redacted so as not to reveal the identity of the nominating source. Notably, MRFF is nominated by one of the founding members of a Nobel Peace Prize-winning humanitarian organization.

November 30, 2011
MRFF Denounces Rep. Rick Womick's (R-TN34) Statement Regarding Muslims in the US Military

On Veterans Day, Rep. Womick calls for purging Muslims from the US Military. MRFF's released statement closed with the admonition that, "Rather than desecrating the memory of fallen US soldiers of the Muslim faith and casting aspersion on the wholly innocent followers of the world's second largest religion, Representative Womick would do well to bow his head in honor of those who are faithfully serving an instrumental role in American Theaters of Operations worldwide, as well as those who have suffered injuries in battle or have made the ultimate sacrifice for those same freedoms which he seeks to discard."

December 7, 2011
MRFF Submits Written Testimony to Joint Senate/House Hearing

MRFF submits written testimony that details the plight of service member clients of the Muslim Faith, victims of Islamophobia in the ranks, to the Joint Hearing of the House of Representatives Committee on Homeland Security and the Senate Committee on Homeland Security and Governmental Affairs: "Homegrown Terrorism: The threat to military communities inside the United States."

December 9, 2011
MRFF and Allies Demand Relocation of Unconstitutionally Placed Religious Displays at Travis Air Force Base

World renowned law firm Jones Day submits a letter on behalf of MRFF to Colonel Dwight C. Somes, Commander, 60th Air Mobility Wing at Travis AFB, demanding an unconstitutionally placed religious display to be relocated from the Base's main gate to the grounds of the Base Chapel. Although the display is not relocated, several significant concessions are made regarding lighting and access to non-Christians, including atheists, at the main gate location. The US Air Force also requests a meeting to discuss the issue with Mikey Weinstein.

January 16, 2012
MRFF's Founder & President Releases Second Book and Announces Book Tour

No Snowflake in an Avalanche: The Military Religious Freedom Foundation, its Battle to Defend the Constitution, and One Family's Courageous War Against Religious Extremism in High Places, published by Rare Bird Books' Vireo imprint, by Michael L. "Mikey" Weinstein and Davin Seay, is released on January 16, 2012. A fourteen city book tour in support of this release is also announced.

January 30, 2012
Rabidly Islamophobic retired Lt. Gen. William G. "Jerry" Boykin Withdraws from West Point Speech

MRFF sends a demand letter to Secretary of the Army John McHugh on January 27, 2012 condemning the outrageous and scandalous decision to invite the rabidly Islamophobic retired Lieutenant General William Boykin to speak before the National Prayer Breakfast at the United States Military Academy at West Point, scheduled for February 8, 2012. MRFF successfully demands rescission of his invitation. This is done on behalf of twenty-seven faculty members and seventy-four cadets, all MRFF clients, and all but seven of which are either Protestant or Roman Catholic.

February 9, 2012
MRFF Demands that Marine Corps Leadership Immediately Investigate Usage of Nazi SS Flag by Marines in Afghanistan

An initial Marine investigation into the matter concludes that troops will not be disciplined because there is no malicious intent. However, Commandant of the United States Marine Corps James Amos issues an official apology and Defense Secretary Leon Panetta pledges to launch an investigation, just one day after MRFF reveals photos to the international press and sends a letter demanding immediate investigation of Marines displaying this notorious, bloodstained symbol. Defense Secretary Leon Panetta tells the Marine Corps to reinvestigate and take appropriate action against the Marine snipers accused of posing with the logo resembling a notorious Nazi symbol.

February 13, 2012
MRFF Exposes Combat Outpost "Aryan" in Afghanistan

After being contacted by ten members of the "ANA" (Afghan National Army) and twenty-one members of the US Armed Forces, MRFF sends a demand letter to Secretary of Defense Leon Panetta seeking the renaming of the facility and an investigation of the circumstances surrounding the initial naming of "Aryan."

February 15, 2012
MRFF Demands Courts-Martial for Head of Defense Information Systems Agency (DISA)

Air Force Lt. Gen. Ronnie Hawkins conducts an all-hands Commander's Call on February 15, 2012 with his subordinate employees at DISA, concluding with the eighteen priorities of "Ronnie's Rules." These rules begin with "Always put God first, and stay within His will" and close with "Always remember that God is good—all the time!" Twenty-one DISA employees, both civilian and military, immediately contact MRFF with one of these employees sending MRFF a copy of Lt. Gen. Hawkins presentation.

March 19, 2012
MRFF Signs Joint Letter to Attorney General Regarding NYPD Surveillance of Muslim Americans

MRFF cosigns a letter to US Attorney General Eric Holder with other civil rights, faith, community, and advocacy groups—over 110 total—expressing deep concern regarding the New York Police Department's well-documented and blanket surveillance of Muslim communities in America without any suspicion of wrong doing and based solely on the faith of the targeted individuals and communities.

March 27, 2012
MRFF Pressure Leads to US Air Force Removing Mandatory Chapel Policy

An active duty CGO (Company Grade Officer 2nd Lt., 1st Lt., Captain) of the US Air Force contacts MRFF seeking assistance when he finds the curriculum of the Squadron Officer School (SOS) contains a chapel attendance mandate. International law firm Jones Day submits a letter on behalf of

MRFF to Secretary of the Air Force Michael Donley and Air Force Chief of Staff Gen. Norton Schwartz demanding removal of language from Air Force training documents that mandates regular chapel attendance as part of the "Spiritual and Ethical Responsibilities" of a commissioned Air Force officer.

In a letter dated April 2, 2012, the Air Force Judge Advocate confirms that the documents containing the chapel attendance mandate have been removed from the curriculum of the Squadron Officer School. On behalf of MRFF and its clients, international law firm Jones Day follows up by sending a letter to the Air Force Judge Advocate reiterating MRFF's demand that the Air Force open a review of mandatory training materials to identify and remove other similarly unconstitutional language. Due to continuing vague responses regarding review of additional mandatory training material, Jones Day files a FOIA (Freedom of Information Act) request on behalf of MRFF on April 26, 2012.

April 26, 2012
MRFF Commends Chairman of the US Joint Chiefs of Staff for Ordering Review and Removal of Anti-Islamic Training Material

MRFF issues a press release supporting the order given on Tuesday, April 24th, 2012 by General

Martin Dempsey, Chairman of the United States Joint Chiefs of Staff, that all training and educational materials throughout the military be immediately reviewed to ensure that no anti-Muslim or anti-Islam references or content remain. This unprecedented review is the result of a belated discovery at the Joint Forces Staff College (JFSC) in Norfolk, VA. In the elective class "Perspectives on Islam and Islamic Radicalism," officers from all four branches of the military are indoctrinated with vile Islamophobic programs masquerading as "antiterrorist" education. According to Pentagon spokesman Navy Capt. John Kirby, the course contains a PowerPoint slide stating that "the United States is at war with Islam and we ought to just recognize that."

For years, MRFF has sounded urgent alarm bells regarding content taught at the Joint Forces Staff College. In June 2007, career Islamophobic extremist and shady Lebanese fundamentalist Christian evangelical, Brigitte Gabriel, delivers a lecture before the JFSC where she states that there is no such thing as a "moderate Muslim" and that "America and the West are doomed to failure in this war unless they stand up and identify the real enemy: Islam." According to reports, this lecture is presented "as part of the school's Islam elective."

In February 2008, self-proclaimed "ex-terrorist" and "ex-Muslim" fundamentalist Christian minstrels Walid Shoebat, Zachariah Anani, and Kamal Saleem are paid $13,000 to speak before the 50th Annual Academy Assembly at the USAFA in Colorado Springs, CO on the topic of "Dismantling Terrorism: Developing Actionable Solutions for Today's Plague of Violence." At this conference, Walid Shoebat disgustingly states: "We have to kill Islam." MRFF responds by demanding equal time to counter these frauds, resulting in speaking appearances at USAFA for MRFF Advisory Board Member and Islam Scholar Reza Aslan, MRFF Board member and former Ambassador Joseph C. Wilson IV, and MRFF founder and President Mikey Weinstein.

May 10, 2012
MRFF Condemns and Submits FOIA Regarding Joint Forces Staff College (JFSC) Training Which Advocates Waging 'Total War' Against Muslim Civilian Populations

JFSC faculty member Army Lt. Col. Matthew A. Dooley, introduces a presentation to officers from all four branches of the US Military entitled, "'So What Can We Do?' A Counter-Jihad Op Design Model" (July, 2011) including the following statements/recommendations for consideration:

The model asserts Islam has already declared war on the West, and the United States specifically, as is demonstrable with over thirty years of violent history. It is, therefore, illogical to continue along our current global strategy models that presume there are always possible options for common ground and detent with the Muslim Umma with waging near "total war."

This would leave open the option once again of taking war to a civilian population wherever necessary (the historical precedents of Dresden, Tokyo, Hiroshima, Nagasaki being applicable to the Mecca and Medina destruction DP [decision point] in Phase III.)

This presentation is delivered as part of the "Perspective on Islam and Islamic Radicalism" course of the JFSC.

MRFF submits a Freedom of Information Act (FOIA) request to the President of the National Defense University, the Commandant of the Joint Forces Staff College, and the Secretary of the DoD for all agency documents pertaining to all training materials, documents, and communications associated with the Perspectives on Islam course and Lt. Col. Dooley's presentation.

Gen. Martin Dempsey, Chairman of the Joint Chiefs, orders the entire US military to remove all anti-Islamic content from its training materials.

May 24, 2012

MRFF Action Leads to Renaming of Marine Fighter Attack Squadron 122 (VMFA-122)

On April 17, 2012 MRFF initially challenges a Marine fighter squadron decision on renaming from the "Werewolves" to the "Crusaders." The squadron, based in Beaufort, S.C., uses the Crusaders symbol from 1958 to 2008, when Lt. Col. William Lieblein points out that imagery invoking the Christian conquest and colonization of Muslim nations during the Middle Ages is counterproductive to the US presence across the Arab and Islamic world. In a letter on May 23, 2012 to Navy Secretary, Ray Mabus, and Commandant of the Marine Corps, General James F. Amos, MRFF threatens legal action to force a change in the squadron name. MRFF also submits a Freedom of Information Act request for all communication and documentation related to the return of the squadron's name from "Werewolves" to "Crusaders."

VMFA-122 is ordered to reverse the decision, and to return to identifying itself as "Werewolves." The deputy commandant for aviation directs VMFA-122 to maintain the unit identification as the "Werewolves," according to Marine Corps public information officer Lt. Col. Joseph Plenzler. To discourage similar actions in the future,

MRFF demands prosecution of those who make the decision to rename the squadron the "Crusaders," along with a full accounting of the resulting costs to US taxpayers.

June 5, 2012
Space and Missile Systems Center "Industry Days" Rescheduled After MRFF Intervenes on Behalf of Clients

During Space and Missile Systems Center (SMSC) Industry Days, industry members are invited to learn about what's new and what's next at the Space and Missile Systems Center, which is located at the Los Angeles Air Force Base. The 2012 Event is scheduled for September 25, 2012 through September 27, 2012 at exactly the same time that Jewish people observe what is considered the holiest day of their calendar, Yom Kippur, or the Day of Atonement. MRFF steps in on behalf of twenty-seven clients, sixteen of whom are Jewish, after their repeated attempts to bring the conflict to the attention of leadership fell on deaf ears and their requests for rescheduling were ignored. Based on MRFFs direct intervention, Doug Loverro, Executive Director of the SMSC, directly emails MRFF to state that, "We intend to change the dates for SMC Industry days to deconflict it with Yom Kippur."

June 11, 2012

US Military Emblems No Longer Allowed on Holman Military Bibles

Over the course of a few years, MRFF receives nearly 2,000 complaints about Bibles that are displayed and sold in base exchanges and other stores on military bases. This raises fears among military personnel that, in the words of an anonymous US Air Force Judge Advocate, it's "a big step towards establishing the Holman Christian Standard Bible as the official religious text of the military services of the United States." The dangerous nature of an official endorsement of Bibles by the US Military is made clear by the fact that the Holman translation does not include those texts purged from the Bible during the Protestant Reformation which are still included in Roman Catholic and Eastern Orthodox editions of the Holy Bible. Entitled "The Soldier's Bible," "Sailor's Bible," "Marine's Bible," and "Airman's Bible," respectively, the HSBC Bibles contain material merging Evangelical symbolism and theology with national and military iconography and anthems.

In addition to the constitutional issue of allowing the use of official US military emblems on any Bible, these Holman military Bibles also contain a lengthy section of essays and other information promoting the Officers' Christian Fellowship (OCF), an organization of about 15,000 military officers who think the real duty of a military officer is to raise up "a spiritually transformed military, with ambassadors for Christ in uniform, empowered by the Holy Spirit."

Following direct efforts by MRFF on behalf of its clients, all four branches of the US Military have now revoked their approval of the Military series of Holman Christian Standard Bibles (HCSB).

August 16, 2012
MRFF Exposes Adjutant General of the State of Indiana Fundraising for Christian Fundamentalist Group While in Uniform

On behalf of thirty-one MRFF clients, and members of the Indiana Army and Air National Guard, MRFF sends a letter on August 16, 2012 to the Chief of the National Guard Bureau, General Craig R. McKinley demanding that he order Major General R. Martin Umbarger and Army Chaplain (Major) Doug Hedrick to cease and desist from any further violations of DoD and/or UCMJ mandates regarding their overt endorsement of and participation in the parachurch proselytizing organization Centurion's Watch. MRFF also demands Maj. General Umbarger, Chaplain (Major)

Hedrick, and any and all other complicit individuals be severely punished accordingly.

Centurion's Watch (CW) is a faith-based nonprofit organization with a clear proselytizing mission within the U.S Military ("...that every military family will hear the life-transforming message of Jesus Christ regarding how they can experience strong, healthy, marriage relationships"). Adjutant General of the State of Indiana, Major General R. Martin Umbarger appears in a September 2011 fundraising video appeal, in uniform, on behalf of CW. Additionally, CW's apparent founder and director is Army Chaplain (Major) Doug Hedrick. Both actions represent a number of nontrivial potential DoD & UCMJ violations and conflicts of interest.

August 24, 2012
MRFF Exposes "Longitudinal Character Study" at the US Military Academy at West Point as an Unconstitutional Religious Test

Forty-two MRFF clients at West Point, thirty-five of whom are Academy cadets, and seven of whom are members of the faculty, reach out to MRFF following the administration of the "Longitudinal Character Study" at West Point. Out of these forty-two MRFF clients, thirty-five are practicing Christians. The clients attest to the fact that the survey is a part of the overall religious pressure at the prestigious US Military Academy. Of the eighty-nine questions sent to members of the Class of 2013, a half-dozen questions relating to faith and spirituality represent an unconstitutional test of religious preference. On August 24, 2012, MRFF President and Founder Mikey Weinstein issues a letter to Lieutenant General David H. Huntoon, Superintendent of the United States Military Academy at West Point forcefully demanding that the unconstitutional "Religious Test" at West Point be put to an end.

August 27, 2012

Editorial in *Air Force Times* Credits Mikey Weinstein and MRFF as Integral to Adoption of "Government Neutrality Regarding Religion" Standards in Air Force Instruction 1-1

Air Force Instruction 1-1 is published on August 7, 2012 by order of the Secretary of the Air Force. AFI 1-1 clearly states that: "Compliance With This Publication Is Mandatory." Section 2.11 of AFI 1-1 pertains to maintenance of religious neutrality: 2.11. Government Neutrality Regarding Religion. Leaders at all levels must balance constitutional protections for an individual's free exercise of religion or other personal beliefs and the constitutional prohibition against governmental establishment of religion. For example, they must avoid the actual or apparent use of their position to promote their personal religious beliefs to their subordinates or to extend preferential treatment for any religion. Commanders or supervisors who engage in such behavior may cause members to doubt their impartiality and objectivity. The potential result is a degradation of the unit's morale, good order, and discipline. Airmen, especially commanders and supervisors, must ensure that in exercising their right of religious free expression, they do not degrade morale, good order, and discipline in the Air Force or degrade the trust and confidence that the public has in the United States Air Force.

In an editorial published in the *Air Force Times* on August 27, 2012, Air Force veteran and historian Robert F. Dorr states: "As officials confirmed for me—it was mostly because of Weinstein's in-your-face activism that Air Force Instruction 1-1, Section 2.11, came into existence Aug. 7."

September 26, 2012
MRFF Exposes Ongoing Problems with "Jesus Rifles"

In January, 2010, MRFF discovers the abhorrent usage of Bible verses on US Military rifles then immediately selects ABC News *Nightline* program as the vehicle through which to break this astonishing story. As the story goes on to make international mainstream news, military forces in the United States, Canada, New Zealand, Australia, United Kingdom, and Israel all express clear intentions to remove the scriptural references on their weaponry. Even General David Petraeus, Commander of US Central Command, as well as Sen. Carl Levin, Chairman of the Senate Armed Services Committee, make clear statements of their concern over the "Jesus Rifles" travesty. The DoD says that it plans to remove inscriptions from sights that are in storage first, then wait to remove them from the sights on weapons in use in Iraq and Afghanistan—after the deployed units that are using them return home. Although this plan completely ignores the main reason that inscriptions urgently need to be removed, everyone is led to believe that this situation will eventually be resolved.

Nearly three years later, NBCNews.com reports on September 26, 2012 that despite the military's assertion that it's making "good progress," the code remains on many rifles deploying to Afghanistan, which some soldiers argue is endangering their lives by reinforcing suspicions that the United States is waging a crusade against Muslims. MRFF

Founder and President Mikey Weinstein states to NBC that: "It's constitutionally noxious. It's an embarrassment and makes us look exactly like the tenth incarnation of the crusades which launches eight million new jihadist recruiting videos."

September 26, 2012
MRFF Client Exposes US Army Suicide Prevention Sessions Lead to Forced "Mass Christian Prayer"

During an Army-wide stand down for suicide prevention sessions, a Christian chaplain in Texas improperly leads rookie soldiers in a candlelight prayer, an Army instructor says in a formal complaint. Staff Sgt. Victoria Gettman, a lab technician instructor at Fort Sam Houston, informs MRFF that she was among 800 soldiers from the 264th Medical Battalion undergoing resilience training on Sept. 26, 2012. Almost all of the soldiers are fresh out of boot camp and in training for their first job in the Army. Thirty-eight service members at the base, including eleven who were in the room, tell MRFF they are willing to sign a federal complaint against "this unconstitutional disaster." Among the group are twenty-four Christians (Protestants and Roman Catholics), two Jews, and twelve agnostics or atheists.

December 17, 2012
Mikey Weinstein Named to List of 100 Most Influential People in US Defense

MRFF President and Founder, Mikey Weinstein is named to the inaugural 100 Most Influential People in US Defense on December 17, 2012. This list is compiled over five months by more than two dozen reporters and editors representing the world's biggest military newsroom and the award-winning staffs of Gannett Government Media's sector-leading publications: *Defense News, Army Times, Air Force Times, Navy Times, Marine Corps Times, Armed Forces Journal* and *Federal Times.* Inclusion in this list is based on an individuals' personal influence, not just the power that comes with their office. One individual on the list explains the concept of personal influence as "making change, it's not just celebrity." Mikey is credited by *Defense News* as having "driven real change in religious policy throughout the military."

December 27, 2012
MRFF Action Gets Immediate Correction of Inappropriate Proselytization by Unit Commander

MRFF receives the following complaint on December 26, 2012 from an active duty member of the US Navy:

"Our unit commander, [name and rank withheld], asked all of the senior NCOs in our unit including me whether or not we had 'come to Christ yet' at the unit's so-called 'X-mas Party' on board ship held a few days ago. He did it in front of the whole unit. Everyone was intimidated and they all said yes except for me. I just said, 'working on it Skip.' He frowned and I felt bad but thought it was over with. I was mistaken. Today he came by my work station with a bible and a personal written invitation to join his 'bible study.' It meets three times a week. During actual duty hours either late or early. Again in front of the crew I lead."

Based upon this complaint, Mikey Weinstein contacts appropriate US Navy personnel demanding this situation be rectified immediately along with proper disciplinary action against the unit commander. On December 27, 2012, MRFF receives this follow-up response from our client:

"I am the United States Navy sailor, my rank is [rank withheld] stationed on board the aircraft carrier USS [name withheld], CVN- [numerical designation withheld], who contacted you yesterday about being unduly proselytized to by my unit's CO, [name and rank withheld]. I was out of options. Did not know what to do? Talked to my dad (retired Navy) and my wife. They recommended to ask MRFF for the help needed. All I can say is that when my next duty shift started today I was ordered to my CO's CO and his CO was there, too. They apologized for what had happened and told me of the corrective procedures taken against my unit's CO. I cannot reveal what has been done. Wish I could. But let me say that it is so perfect I cannot believe it is going down that way! To fit the "crime" I mean. Neither me nor any of the crew I lead will even have to see our former CO for quite a while. Apparently my problem with him was not the first such time. Yesterday was my worst day in the Navy. But today is my best day thanks to the MRFF! I have never seen such a fast and productive response. Mr. Weinstein and the MRFF, I do not know what you did? But you did it in way less than a day from my contacting you. Just so you know, I am a Protestant. My brother in law is an ordained pastor and he married my wife and me. He also baptized each of our 4 kids. My family and I cannot thank all of you ever enough. I am sending the MRFF url website to every sailor I know on board our vessel and the whole Navy!"

January 7, 2013
MRFF Demands SecDef Investigate and Punish Those Responsible for Distribution of Anti-Semitic Comic Book

On January 6, 2013, MRFF receives a complaint from a US Army Soldier stationed at Camp Arifjan,

Kuwait about a copy of *Manga Messiah* being left under his bunk in a plastic bag bundled with other standard tracts "you find in stacks on every chaplain's desk." According to the complaint, Camp Arifjan is the last stop service members have before entering or leaving Iraq (predrawn) or Afghanistan.

It is quite clear that *Manga Messiah*, for a plethora of incontrovertible reasons, is blatantly anti-Semitic. For instance, one of the main themes of these horrible books is the wretched, age-old libel that Jews are directly responsible for the crucifixion of Jesus Christ and, further still, that Jews have conspiratorially consorted with the devil in that crucifixion "plot" and other nefarious anti-Christian endeavors. MRFF clients do not know whether it is DoD chaplains or our clients' chains of command who are behind the distribution of these bigoted materials. What MRFF does know is that these comic books have been distributed liberally across all the service branches and on military bases and naval vessels all over the world including the combat zones of Afghanistan, Iraq, and at many other US armed forces bases in the Area of Responsibility (AOR).

On January 7, 2013, MRFF sends a letter to US Secretary of Defense Leon Panetta demanding an expeditious and comprehensive investigation into this sordid matter. MRFF also demands swift and aggressive punishment for all responsible DoD personnel that have either directly or indirectly facilitated the distribution of these heinous *Manga Messiah* comic books.

January 10, 2013
US Naval Academy Officer's Christian Fellowship Removes Slogan from Website After MRFF FOIA Request

For many years, the "purpose" statement of the Officers' Christian Fellowship (OCF), an organization of over 15,000 fundamentalist Christian officers operating throughout the military, was: "A spiritually transformed military, with ambassadors for Christ in uniform, empowered by the Holy Spirit." MRFF submitted a FOIA request to find out who was responsible for this blatant proclamation of a purpose so antithetical to the purpose of training future officers at the service academies.

In the wake of MRFF's FOIA request, the OCF page on the Naval Academy's website is changed to: "Our purpose is to glorify God by uniting Christian midshipmen for Biblical fellowship and outreach, equipping and encouraging them to minister effectively in the military society."

This does not mean OCF has actually changed its purpose in trying to turn the US military into a force of "ambassadors for Christ in uniform," a statement that should give everybody a pretty good idea of the OCF's attitude towards the Constitution, and their desire to circumvent it to convert the military. However, it does mean that with continued pressure by MRFF, small incremental victories will continue to turn the tide against the threat to national security that this type of activity creates.

January 15, 2013
MRFF Announces Recipients of the Courageous Sacrifice Scholarship for Constitutional Defense and the Freedom's Promise Research Grant for the Advancement of Religious Liberty on January 15, 2013

The Courageous Sacrifice Scholarship for Constitutional Defense is meant to honor those service members who have displayed academic excellence and bravery in fighting to safeguard the foundational American values which every service member has sworn an oath to defend. The recipient of this $2000 scholarship is Blake Page, former West Point cadet who was compelled to resign from the United States Military Academy by the pervasive Christian fundamentalist presence at the Academy—but not before blowing the lid off of the Christian fundamentalist regime at West Point.

The Freedom's Promise Research Grant for the Advancement of Religious Liberty is a $2000 gift meant to fund scholarly research that reflects MRFF's mission. MRFF could think of no more deserving candidate for this tribute than Doctor David Mullin, a former associate professor of economics at the USAFA. Dr. Mullin gained the ire of certain USAFA administrators for his forthright defense of cadets' constitutionally assured rights to carry on their studies unmolested by coercive Christian proselytization.

February 13, 2013
MRFF Demands Corrective & Punitive Action When USAFA Promotes Reprehensible Homophobic Website as Source for Jewish Holiday Information

MRFF submitts a letter to General Mark A. Welsh III, Chief of Staff, United States Air Force, demanding that links to the website (jewfaq.org) no longer be used as educational reference points for matters of the Jewish faith and that those parties responsible face swift and decisive corrective measures. MRFF followed this with erecting a billboard on March 5, 2013 in Colorado Springs, CO (home of USAFA) and a protest rally on March 8, 2013 attended by approximately sixty-five people. Both events received significant coverage which finally led USAFA to "delink" this offensive website.

March 14, 2013

Lawrence Wilkerson, Former Chief of Staff to Sec. of State Colin Powell, Joins MRFF Advisory Board Statement from Col. Wilkerson

"Inside the Washington Beltway today, everyone thinks the budget is the primary issue for the military. It isn't. Far more serious for the health of America's Armed Forces are two issues ripping at their very soul: sexual assault and the lack of religious freedom. Besides breaking the law, the first destroys irreparably the bond so important to military servicemembers; the second contains the potential to destroy the Constitution. I joined the Advisory Board of the Military Religious Freedom Foundation to stand alongside Mikey Weinstein and do my part in preventing that destruction."

April 23, 2013

MRFF Meets with Pentagon Officials Regarding Implementation of Religious Neutrality Standards

MRFF President/Founder Mikey Weinstein, MRFF Board Member Ambassador Joseph Wilson, and MRFF Advisory Board Member Colonel (ret.) Lawrence Wilkerson meet with a Pentagon group that includes several generals and a military chaplain to discuss religious neutrality issues within the US Military.

April 29, 2013

MRFF Demands Invitation to Discredited Christian Fundamentalist Historian David Barton be Rescinded

On Monday, April 29, 2013, MRFF submits a letter of demand to Secretary of Defense Chuck Hagel regarding the highly inappropriate nature of a planned speaking event featuring "historian" David Barton. Mr. Barton is an egregiously inappropriate speaker for this or any other military event for the following three reasons:

1) His open contempt for and denigration of the President and other government officials.

2) His denigration of faith groups other than his own.

3) His revisionism of American history.

Article 88 of the Uniform Code of Military Justice (UCMJ) states that:

"Any commissioned officer who uses contemptuous words against the President, the Vice President, Congress, the Secretary of Defense, the Secretary of a military department, the Secretary of Transportation, or the Governor or legislature of any State, Territory, Commonwealth, or possession in which he is on duty or present shall be punished as a court-martial may direct."

Although Mr. Barton is not himself in the military, the invitation for him to speak at this military event can be considered nothing less than the condoning and endorsement of statements that if made by the officer(s) who invited him to speak would be punishable by their court-martial.

May 10, 2013
MRFF Receives First Ever Approval to Participate in the Combined Federal Campaign (CFC)

MRFF receives approval from the CFC Director of the US Office of Personnel Management on May 10, 2013 to participate in the 2013 CFC fall campaign. CFC is the world's largest and most successful annual workplace charity campaign, with almost 200 CFC campaigns throughout the country and overseas raising millions of dollars each year. The CFC Annual Fall Campaign is a significant event for all federal civilian and military employees. The impact of MRFF's acceptance into the 2013 CFC is best described by a MRFF client:

"Others may not understand the impact this has, but I do. When the annual CFC drive starts, many (MANY) conversations occur in Ready Rooms, squadron bars, the duty desk, etc etc etc...about what is on 'the list' and what is not. I've been there, done that, and 'have the T-shirt' so to speak. This is HUGE. This is a true grass roots visceral level indictment of belief on soooooo many levels for soooooo many folks in the military. Not only is this about 'show me the money'...this is about day to day conversation. A conversation that is long overdue."

May 31, 2013
MRFF Forces Removal of Overtly Religious Artwork from Dining Hall at Mountain Home AFB

MRFF is contacted by a noncommissioned officer (NCO) from Mountain Home Air Force Base, acting as the spokesperson for a group of twenty-two airmen (seventeen of the twenty-two are Christians, both Catholic and Protestant) who want this repugnant piece of artwork removed. Mikey Weinstein immediately calls the Pentagon and gives the Air Force an hour to take action. By the time Mikey talks to the Wing Commander at the base a few minutes later, the Wing Commander has already been contacted by the Pentagon. Fifty-six minutes after his call to the Pentagon, the image of the crusader, with its odious melding of the crusader flag with the American flag, has been removed from the dining hall. The Wing Commander at Mountain Home Air Force Base says he will be ordering another "Health & Welfare" inspection to rid his base of anything else like what had been hanging in the dining hall.

June 3, 2013
MRFF Receives Assurance from USAFA to Improve Briefing & Preparation of Commissioning Ceremony Speakers

During an official USAFA fifty-year commissioning ceremony for USAFA Cadet Squadron 13 on Tuesday, May 28, 2013, Lt. Gen. James A. Fain (USAF-Ret.), Class of 1963, implores graduates to "help return this country to the Christian values it was founded on." MRFF receives a client complaint regarding this perverted interpretation of both our nation's history and current events while appealing for newly commissioned officers to lend their support to the ongoing assault on our democratic values and the attempt to replace them with a Christian theocracy. After presenting this complaint to USAFA officials, Mikey Weinstein receives, on June 3, 2013, both an agreement on the inappropriate nature of these comments and an assurance that the Vice Commandant (for climate and culture) is meeting soon with the Association of Graduates (AOG) to find out what sort of prebrief/prep the fifty-year class commissioning ceremony speakers and representatives are given prior to showing up and (in some cases) speaking at these events. A staff member of the USAFA Superintendent's Office serving as liaison to the USAFA AOG states:

"The purpose of the 50-year class members' presence at commissioning ceremonies is to present each about-to-graduate cadet with a set of 2Lt bars as a gift from the older class to the younger class. When the AOG briefed the speakers, we primarily spoke about the importance of brevity and of ensuring they didn't deflect the focus from the graduating cadets, as well as suggesting they emphasize the link between their two classes in the Long Blue Line. We didn't imagine anyone would make remarks such as these—we've had no problems with legacy class speakers at commissioning ceremonies in the past. We'll be much more aggressive in the future in instructing these speakers regarding what they can and cannot say—no politics, no religion, no social commentary. The AOG obviously can't promise that something similar won't happen in the future, but we'll do everything we can to prevent it."

June 17, 2013
MRFF's Unprecedented Success Brings Attempt at Congressional Retaliation

On June 13, 2013, Congressman Tim Huelskamp (R-KS) introduces an amendment to the FY2014 National Defense Authorization Act. Huelskamp's amendment, with the heading "Meetings with Respect to Religious Liberty," is passed by a voice vote in the House. Congressman Huel-skamp, in a press release on his website, makes no secret that the sole purpose of his amendment was to stop one man—Military Religious Freedom Foundation (MRFF) founder and president Mikey Weinstein—from "secretly" (or at least as secretly as being reported in *The Washington Post* can be) meeting with military officials at the Pentagon.

After extensive analysis by MRFF's Senior Research Director, Chris Rodda, of the reasonable application of the specific language contained in the proposed amendment, MRFF issues a press release on June 17, 2013 in full support of this proposed amendment. MRFF's support of this proposed amendment is based on a long standing desire to expose the countless meetings that have no doubt occurred, and continue to occur, between military officials and civilians from the various fundamentalist Christian parachurch organizations. These meetings have led to:

· Civilian fundamentalist Christian organizations and individuals that are funded by DoD contracts to bring the troops to Jesus.

· Civilian fundamentalist Christian youth ministries that are granted permission to operate on military installations for the purpose of stalking and converting the children of "unchurched" military personnel, and the civilians involved in the implementation of the military-wide glut of "spiritual fitness" tests and programs.

Congressman Huelskamp's amendment, unintended or not, provides MRFF with the avenue to uncover the specific actions taken in developing and implementing these, and many more, unconstitutional religious programs within the US Military.

July 3, 2013
MRFF's Action on Behalf of Clients Quickly Produces Corrective Action Regarding Sectarian Prayer During Official Ceremony at US Military Research Facility

A spokesperson for a group of forty service members and military contractors (thirty-two being either Protestant or Catholic) at a US Military research facility contacts MRFF with a complaint that a ceremony with required attendance included a speaker who invoked religious references to prayer and worship that clearly applies to certain religious groups and not all in attendance. The spokesperson states that he contacted MRFF on behalf of himself and others "after being given the impression that I must conform to a narrow range of religious beliefs (or any belief at all, as I am non-religious) in order to be considered patriotic."

MRFF President and Founder, Mikey Weinstein, immediately contacts the commanding officer of the facility on behalf of these MRFF clients to resolve this situation. In response, the commanding officer of the research facility issued the following statement to those under his command:

Last week during the...ceremony, I witnessed an example of exclusion instead of inclusion that was inappropriate, in my view. During the invocation, the speaker invoked religious references to prayer and worship that clearly applied to certain religious groups and not all in attendance. I was uncomfortable with the choice of words as were many others. That is not appropriate for official military ceremonies. There is a place for invocations by chaplains in military ceremonies. Those secular or nondenominational invocations must be meaningful for all in attendance and must not make attendees uncomfortable and unable to enjoy the important event. Exclusionary religious invocations are not appropriate at...official events...

July 23, 2013
MRFF Action Forces Immediate Removal of Chaplain's Statement Denigrating Military Service of Atheists

Lt. Col. Kenneth Reyes, installation Chaplain at Joint Base Elmendorf-Richardson (JBER) posts an article to the JBER official website entitled, "Chaplain's Corner: 'No atheists in foxholes': Chaplains gave all in World War II." This article contains the redundant use of the bigoted, religious supremacist phrase, "no atheists in foxholes," and defiles the dignity of service members by telling them that regardless of their personally held philosophical beliefs they must have faith. On behalf of forty-two clients at JBER, Blake Page (Special Assistant to MRFF President) contacts the commanding officer of JBER demanding appropriate action be taken to remove this article from JBER's official website and that punitive measures and negative counseling be produced for all those involved in the production, approval, and dissemination of Lt. Col. Reyes' message of religious supremacy and disrespect toward the nonreligious. The article is immediately removed and MRFF awaits confirmation on additional corrective action being taken to prevent similar future incidents.

August 26, 2013
MRFF Meets with Superintendent/Commanding General of US Military Academy (West Point) to Discuss Religious Respect Problems and Related Constitutional Issues

On Monday, August 26, 2013, MRFF Founder and President Mikey Weinstein and longtime MRFF ally Lt. Gen. William T. Lord (USAF ret.) meet with

Lt. Gen. Robert L. Caslen Jr., newly appointed Superintendent and Commanding General at West Point. This meeting holds particularly remarkable significance due to well-publicized past conflicts between MRFF and Lt. Gen. Caslen created by Lt. Gen Caslen's direct involvement in Christian Dominionist activities within the US Military. These include appearing, in uniform, in the notorious Pentagon/Christian Embassy proselytizing video in 2006 and serving as President of the uber-fundamentalist Officers' Christian Fellowship organization.

MRFF requests this meeting discuss serious religious respect problems and a myriad of related Constitutional religious issues at West Point where MRFF currently has 177 clients amongst the Academy's cadets, faculty, and staff (137 of them practicing Christians). The success of this meeting (and remarkable proof of the Superintendent's true dignity, honesty, diligence, and worth) is effectively encapsulated in subsequent correspondence on August 27, 2013 with Lt. Gen. Caslen stating:

I look forward to our future interactions as we at the United States Military Academy strive to develop leaders of character who see themselves, and all those whom they encounter, as persons of dignity and worth.

This language was suggested by MRFF as an alternative to a solely faith-based sense of leadership dignity and worth among West Point cadets.

September 20, 2013

Obama Administration Responds to a "We The People" White House Petition by Citing Changes in "Spiritual Fitness" Test Language and Applicability Recommended by MRFF

MRFF long disagrees with the methodology of the Comprehensive Soldier Fitness (CSF) Program's Soldier Fitness Tracker (SFT) and Global Assessment Tool (GAT) which requires responses by enlisted soldiers to statements such as "I am a spiritual person" and "I believe there is a purpose for my life." These statements are geared toward soldiers that hold particular religious beliefs, while punishing soldiers who do not share those beliefs, particularly atheists and nontheists. Soldiers who fail to perform sufficiently well on the spirituality component of the SFT are required to spend extra time and effort in undergoing supplemental "spiritual training" to become "more spiritual" through the use of CSF Training Modules or whatever other "remedial" instruction their commanders prescribe. It is MRFF's understanding that the military's position is that soldiers are not fit for duty if they do not attain an adequate "spiritual fitness" score on the spirituality component of the SFT and GAT, or did not undergo required remedial training in spirituality. On December 29, 2010, the international law firm Jones Day, on behalf of MRFF and its client Sgt. Justin Griffith, files a Freedom of Information Act (FOIA) request with the Department of Army regarding the development and implementation of the spiritual well-being component of the Comprehensive Soldier Fitness program's Soldier Fitness Tracker (SFT) and Global Assessment Tool (GAT). On December 30, 2010, Jones Day also files a demand with the Secretary of the Army and the Army Chief of Staff to cease and desist its policy of administering the spiritual component of the Comprehensive Soldier Fitness (CSF) Program's Soldier Fitness Tracker (SFT) and Global Assessment Tool (GAT) to enlisted men and women and immediately discontinue all mandatory follow-up to that component of the test.

In response to these concerns, MRFF President and Founder Mikey Weinstein is invited to meet with Dept. of Defense officials responsible for development and implementation of the SFT/GAT in Washington, DC. MRFF invites the Rev. Dr. C. Welton Gaddy, President of Interfaith Alliance to attend this meeting in support of MRFF's position.

On October 1, 2011, Dustin Chalker, non-Theist Affairs Advisor for MRFF, initiates a petition on the White House "We The People" website entitled, "End the Military's Discrimination against

Non-Religious Service Members." On September 20, 2013, The White House respondes to this petition, in part, with this language:

The spiritual dimension questions in the Global Assessment Tool were changed in September 2012 in order to reflect more accurately the perspectives of both religious and nonreligious users. These are the current measures by which users self assess:

I am a person of dignity and worth.

My life has meaning.

I believe that in some way my life is closely connected to all humanity and all the world.

The job I am doing in the military has enduring meaning.

I believe there is a purpose for my life.

It is also important to understand the results of the self-assessment survey are only for the soldier, and are not shared with the command or with any other person. This survey is simply a resiliency tool to help soldiers self-identify areas where they may need additional emphasis in their lives. Soldiers are free to disregard the feedback from the automated program if they feel that it does not apply to them, and no training on spiritual fitness is mandatory.

This response from the Obama Administration reflects specific language ("I am a person of dignity and worth") proposed by MRFF in conjunction with Rev. Dr. C. Welton Gaddy. This response also addresses MRFF concerns about the religious and mandatory nature of the "Spiritual Fitness" test as originally implemented.

September 23, 2013
MRFF Submits FOIA Request Demanding All Records Pertaining to Meeting Between Dept. of Defense Officials and Christian Dominionist Leaders

The Military Religious Freedom Foundation has long observed a continued cozy and incestuous relationship between an activist segment of the highest echelons of the Pentagon and noxious fundamentalist Christian organizations. To uncover details regarding this relationship, MRFF submits a FOIA (Freedom of Information Act) request on September 23, 2013 demanding:

All correspondence, emails, or other records related to the September 12, 2013 meeting at the Pentagon between representatives of the "Restore Military Religious Freedom Coalition" and any Air Force or other DoD personnel, including but not limited to those present at the meeting.

All other correspondence, emails, or other records on any subject between representatives of the "Restore Military Religious Freedom Coalition" and/or its constituent member organizations (including but not limited to the Alliance Defending Freedom, the American Family

Association, Chaplain Alliance for Religious Liberty, and the Family Research Council) and any Air Force or other DoD personnel.

October 3, 2013
MRFF Exposes Close Ties Between Dominionist Groups Meeting with DoD Officials and Fundamentalist Leader Calling for Military Takeover of US Government

On October 3, 2013, MRFF Senior Research Director Chris Rodda reports in *The Huffington Post* and DailyKos on the extremely close ties between the Restore Military Religious Freedom (RMRF) coalition, RMRF coalition member the Family Research Council, and Rick Joyner, the head of MorningStar Ministries/Heritage International Ministries who proposes a "military takeover" of the US Government on September 30, 2013. Lt. Gen. (Ret.) William G. "Jerry" Boykin, who serves as the Family Research Council's Executive Vice President, appeared on Rick Joyner's *Prophetic Perspectives on Current Events* for four of the five episodes in the week leading up to his September 30 proposal for a military takeover of the government. MRFF works to uncover additional information regarding the relationship between these religious dominionist leaders and DoD officials with a FOIA request filed on September 23, 2013 regarding a September 12, 2013 meeting between representatives of the RMRF and the DoD.

October 8, 2013
DoD Officials Responsible for US Army Comprehensive Soldier and Family Fitness Program Seek MRFF's Direct Input

Lt. Colonel Chaplain Stephen W. Austin contacts MRFF President and Founder Mikey Weinstein on October 8, 2013 regarding initial development and implementation of a spirit(ual) dimension component to a US Army soldier resilience platform called ArmyFit. Lt. Col. Austin requests MRFF's advice and review "as we progress in the development of this dimension. Your opinion matters and we would like to work collaboratively on a topic that is clearly complex and sensitive."

This request comes after Mikey is flown at government expense to Washington, DC to meet with Pentagon officials in 2012 to discuss MRFF's concerns regarding "spiritual fitness" testing. MRFF had previously filed objections on behalf of its clients and was preparing an aggressive federal class action lawsuit (through the Jones Day law firm) challenging the Army's "spiritual fitness" testing as it existed at that time.

October 18, 2013

USAFA Superintendent Removes "Prep School" Poster Containing Religious Oath After Being Contacted by MRFF

The Air Force Academy Honor Code ("We Will Not Lie, Steal Or Cheat, Nor Tolerate Among Us Anyone Who Does") is formally adopted in 1956 by the first graduating class, the Class of 1959. It was then, and continues to be today, a minimum standard of conduct which cadets expect of themselves and their fellow cadets. MRFF President and Founder Mikey Weinstein receives a picture of a poster displayed at the USAFA Prep School that contains the Academy's honor code followed with an addendum stating: "Furthermore, I resolve to do my duty and live honorably so help me God."

Mikey immediately contacts USAFA Vice Superintendent Colonel Tamra L. Rank regarding this blatant attempt to introduce a religious element into the approved honor code. Sixty-eight minutes later, USAFA Superintendent Lt. Gen. Michelle Johnson emails Mikey with the following statement:

Thanks for taking the time to talk with my Vice about this matter. This Honor Oath is one of the new things since my graduation, evidently in about 1984. Col Miller was able to bring together the Prep School and other entities on base to put together a way ahead. We've al-

ready directed the Honor Review Committee to fix this next week when they meet. The Prep School poster has been taken down.

November 18, 2013
MRFF Continues Aggressive Campaign Against Ongoing Christian Fundamentalist Extremism at the USAFA

In October 2013, MRFF posts a billboard along one of the busiest thoroughfares in Colorado Springs, CO. MRFF's purpose is to protest the continued usage of unconstitutional religious tests at the USAFA, namely the usage of the phrase, "So Help Me God," within its honor oath. Neither of the Academy's sister service schools, West Point or Annapolis, use that phrase in their respective honor codes. This billboard displays the presidential oath taken by George Washington, which did not include the religious test phrase in question, and asks: "This oath was good enough for George Washington. Why not the Air Force Academy?"

A second billboard is erected on November 18, 2013 focusing on a statement made by a leader at USAFA that, "I am on staff at USAFA and will talk about Jesus Christ my Lord and savior to everyone that I work with." This second billboard is erected in response to the Academy issuing a statement defending and exonerating the USAFA leader, stating that the hate mail [containing the leader's statement] was sent "in his personal capacity," and that "no action is being taken against the individual." This billboard is accompanied with the release of a thirty-second video containing the USAFA leaders proselytizing statement along with MRFF statement that, "The United States Air Force Academy has become a fundamentalist Christian military ministry." This video ad began airing November 19 in Colorado Springs, where the academy is located; and Pueblo, Colo.

November 19, 2013
MRFF Demands USAFA Immediately Fire "ex-Gay" Fundamentalist Christian Who Claimed He Could "Cure" Gays

Notorious antigay bigot Dr. Mike Rosebush is a former vice president of the rabidly fundamentalist Christian, Colorado Springs based Focus on the Family, one of the foremost antigay organizations in the country. Additionally, Rosebush has also been a clinical member of NARTH (the National Association for Research & Therapy of Homosexuality). Rosebush has gained fame and notoriety by taking insipid quack science to ever-lower depths of absurdity. Indeed, the American Psychological Association (APA), in its "Resolution on Appropriate Affirmative Responses to Sexual Orientation Distress and Change Efforts," has taken great pains to underscore such "therapy" as merely the expression of prejudice and discrimination, with a basis in ignorance and the distortion or active disdain of scientific data. Even Exodus International, the organization for which Rosebush served as Professional Counselors' Network director, has publicly apologized for the harm caused by the espousal of the patently false notion that homosexuals can be "cured."

Upon learning that the USAFA is employing this antigay bigot, MRFF immediately sends a letter on behalf of its twenty-seven lesbian/gay/bisexual (LGB) clients at USAFA to Acting Secretary of the Air Force, Eric Fanning. In this letter, MRFF demands that USAFA exercise its responsibility towards the civil rights and protections of cadets, staff, and faculty, and immediately terminate the employment of "ex-gay" fraudster Dr. Mike Rosebush. MRFF responds to USAFA efforts to paint a "happy face" on the widely-reported environment of fundamentalist Christian religious oppression and homophobia by posting the third billboard at USAFA's doorstep in Colorado Springs, CO, within the span of little over a month.

December 6, 2013
US Air Force Relocates Unconstitutional Sectarian Religious Display

MRFF is alerted by clients of a sectarian nativity scene that had been placed at Shaw Air Force Base. This in and of itself is not a problem. However, it isn't within the vicinity of a chapel and isn't part of a scene designed to accommodate all religious preferences, or no preferences, aboard the base. As such, this religious display constitutes a direct violation of the US Constitution as well as a violation of Air Force Instruction 1-1 Section 2.11. Within two and a half hours of being contacted by MRFF, Shaw Air Force Base leaders agree with MRFF and have the display removed to a more appropriate location.

December 14, 2013
MRFF Action Results in Swift Discipline by State National Guard Commanding Officer for Religious Discrimination, Intimidation, and Retribution

Mikey Weinstein is contacted in late November 2013 by a Jewish member of a State Defense Force regarding specific actions taken against him by his chain of command in response to his religious beliefs. After meeting with Mikey and MRFF's Client to discuss the situation, the commanding officer (Brigadier General) of the State's National Guard initiates an investigation into the claims made. As a result of the investigation, the commanding officer takes the following disciplinary actions:

1. BG is fired and a letter goes into his file stating that he cannot return.

2. COL is fired and a letter goes into his file stating that he cannot return.

3. COL is removed from Commander slot and will undergo training.

4. MAJ was reduced in rank back to SGM and will possibly have another strip removed from him.

5. MAJ had a letter placed in his file that he cannot return.

6. COL will not be taking the commander slot.

7. MRFF's Client is advised that he will retain his posting and rank of those listed.

MRFF strongly commends such swift and decisive action as the exact type of leadership necessary to effectively address ongoing un-Constitutional activity and environment within the US Armed Forces.

December 18, 2013
Sectarian Religious Display at GTMO is Relocated to Base Chapel

The Military Religious Freedom Foundation receives an email on Monday night, December 16, 2013, signed by eighteen active-duty service members protesting the Nativity scenes set up at the Guantanamo's Gold Hill and Seaside galleys. After being contacted by MRFF, Capt. J. R. Nettleton, commander of GTMO, moves two Nativity scenes from US troops' cafeterias to the base chapel on December 18, 2013. "The spirit of the Navy's policy on this is, if it's religious, it goes to the chapel," Capt. Nettleton tells the *Miami Herald* after a day of controversy. "It's more appropriate there."

January 11, 2014
Christian Messaging During Official Functions at Air Force Base Halted After MRFF Involvement

Thirteen active duty Airmen stationed at a mainland US Air Force base contact Mikey Weinstein in mid-December 2013 regarding:

"...an alarming pattern emerging in the [USAF unit's name withheld] group, permitted/encouraged by our Commander that fostered dogmatic Christian language and messages at three official functions within a four week period. This was creating an atmosphere that reeked of sectarian attitudes that implicitly harassed airmen with Christian beliefs that did not conform to these proselytizing messages as well as airmen who held other religious or nonreligious views."

As a result of MRFF's involvement on behalf of these thirteen Airmen, the majority of whom are Christian, the following actions are taken as reported by one of MRFF's clients:

"*Within 2 hours of contacting you, AF general officers at HQ in Washington, DC at the Pentagon were mobilized. Within five hours, the Wing commander had ordered my group commander to account for his/her actions. At the twenty-four hour mark, all commanders on base were called to a crisis meeting to discuss religious neutrality and were required to implement immediate changes that would safeguard religious neutrality. Forty-eight hours later, my group commander was apologizing to the 300+ members of the [USAF unit's name withheld] group.*"

January 29, 2014
MRFF Demand Leads to US Air Force Base Dropping Christian Marriage Video from Mandatory Event

MRFF is contacted on January 27, 2014, by twenty-five Airmen (twenty-four of whom self-identify as either Protestant or Catholic) stationed at Little Rock AFB, Arkansas regarding a mandatory-attendance "Wingman Day" that involves many instructional elements pertaining to Physical, Mental, Social, & Spiritual factors. According to an article in the *Little Rock AFB Combat Airlifter*, the Spiritual element is clearly promoting a Christian religious faith with no alternative means. According to the news article, Team Little Rock is hosting this event with "Christian videos," with one of the modules labeled: "Love Happens: God's Purpose and Plan." Prior to contacting Mikey Weinstein at MRFF for assistance, one of the Airmen representing the group sends an e-mail to the Base Public Affairs office regarding the "mandatory requirements" and asks why they believe they should tell people a healthy marriage requires religion and a certain deity. The response received includes a very vague determent stating, "The video series the Chapel is presenting is on marriage from a religious perspective."

Within two days of being contacted by MRFF, the *Air Force Times* reports Little Rock Air Force Base has dropped an evangelical Christian video series on marriage. Stephen Losey of the *Air Force Times* reports that *AFT* was informed by email from Little Rock AFB spokesman Arlo Taylor that the spiritual pillar will now offer two nondenominational marriage classes on communication and intimacy, among other classes.

March 11, 2014

USAFA Cadet Leader Removes Proselytizing Bible Passage Outside His Room After MRFF Client Complaints

Mikey Weinstein, MRFF President and Founder, is contacted by twenty-nine cadets and four faculty and staff members about the posting of a Christian Bible passage outside the private room of a cadet leader. The passage from Galatians 2: 20, "I have been crucified with Christ and I no longer live, but Christ lives in me," is clearly seen as a violation of Section 2.11 of Air Force Instruction (AFI) 1-1:

2.11. Government Neutrality Regarding Religion. Leaders at all levels must balance constitutional protections for an individual's free exercise of religion or other personal beliefs and the constitutional prohibition against governmental establishment of religion. *For example, they must avoid the actual or apparent use of their position to promote their personal religious beliefs to their subordinates* [emphasis added] to extend preferential treatment for any religion. Commanders or supervisors who engage in such behavior may cause members to doubt their impartiality and objectivity. The potential result is a degradation of the unit's morale, good order, and discipline. Airmen, especially commanders and supervisors, must ensure that in exercising their right of religious free expression, they do not degrade morale, good order, and discipline in the Air Force or degrade the trust and confidence that the public has in the United States Air Force.

The passage is removed by the cadet just over two hours after this conflict is brought to his attention by USAFA leadership. During the predictable media furor that arises from this incident, Mikey clearly and concisely explains MRFF's position on behalf of its clients to numerous media outlets:

"Had it been in his room—not a problem. It's not about the belief. It's about the time, the place, and the manner."

MRFF's position on behalf of its clients is further justified when another client (Christian-Protestant AF Captain) shares the following impressions made by USAF Chief of Chaplains, Maj. Gen. Howard Stendahl on March 31, 2014, before a mandatory mass briefing of about 800 officer-students attending Squadron Officer School (SOS) at Maxwell AFB in Montgomery, Alabama:

· Throughout the course of his speech he emphasized that a chaplain's job is to see to the needs of ALL troops regardless of their faith or lack thereof.

· Given the latest news flood about it, it figured that the first question that was asked was about the hot issue currently surrounding the Air Force Academy's latest religious battle. This is the one with cadets posting Bible scriptures on whiteboards in the Academy's public hallways or dormitories. We were curious to see how Maj. Gen. Stendahl would handle this question. The way in which he chose to answer it was more or less, "Would you post a picture of the last political candidate you voted for outside your office?" He then implied that, of course, you wouldn't. "Would you post a political speech outside of your office?" Once again, he made it clear that, of course you wouldn't. He stressed to us all that "the Air Force is a military organization, not a religious organization."

· Maj. Gen. Stendahl definitely seemed to understand this point and drove it home in his response to the aforementioned question. All of us were very happy to hear him do so and we just thought you and the MRFF would like to know about it since that is the MRFF's position too.

April 3, 2014
MRFF Intervenes on Clients' Behalf to Make Attendance Nonmandatory at Speaking Event by Religious Fundamentalist

Mikey Weinstein, MRFF President and Founder, is contacted by an active duty officer (deployed overseas) on behalf of himself and many fellow service members concerned with mandatory attendance at a speaking event promoted as "moral leadership and spiritual resiliency designed to reinforce the Army Values." The key speaker at this event was scheduled to be Southern Baptist Preacher Dr. Richard Blackaby. The active duty officer contacting MRFF stated:

I was astounded to see some of the things he happily professed: that secularism was the root of all of America's ills, posts denigrating President Obama who is our commander-in-chief, and advocating for a definition of leadership that determined one's success based on how deeply one accepted Jesus Christ as one's personal lord and savior.

MRFF's actions and results in this matter on behalf of its clients in this matter are best summarized a few days later by the active duty officer who originally contacted Mikey:

MRFF immediately went to work for myself and the countless other members of our very large military unit concerned by this potential, serious Constitutional breach as well as violations of military regulations. Very quickly we received the incredible word that, due to MRFF's decisive advocacy on our behalf, all the events were now nonmandatory and that official attendance would not be taken. And throughout the process, my anonymity and the anonymity of my fellow service members was completely protected. Their hard work and dedication has ensured that our civil rights were protected. To my fellow service members out there who face similar kinds of illegal religious dictates from their leadership, based on this recent experience I can say with full confidence that the MRFF will provide you with the outstanding assistance they provided us.

July 28, 2014
MRFF Presentation at NMANG Joint Forces Chaplain Training Event

Mikey Weinstein is invited to speak about issues of religious time, place, and purpose expectations and restrictions on July 28, 2014, at a New Mexico Army National Guard Joint Forces Chaplain Training event. Mikey's presentation is tremendously well received and documented in a thank you letter from Chaplain Lieutenant Colonel Quentin Collins who stated:

Your message was timely in that our members had drawn conclusions as to your methodology and delivery style—strictly from what is painted of you in the media. I only asked that they be open to you and what you were saying. To this end they unanimously agreed, they were stunned that you were not out to "get them."

...You helped launch the training to a level that it has not been before, and to that end I thank you very much.

September 17, 2014
Under Pressure from MRFF and Allies, the US Air Force Rescinds the Unlawful and Coercive Requirement That Enlistees State "So Help Me God" in Their Enlistment Oath

Around August 25, 2014, an airman at Creech Air Force Base seeking to reenlist is informed that he must swear to God in order to do so. Airmen were allowed to omit the phrase until October 2013 when the US Air Force changed their interpretation of 10 USC 502, 5 USC 3331, and Title 32. The legal arm of the American Humanist Association represented this airman in a letter to DoD officials on September 2, 2014.

As a result of the treatment of the airman at Creech AFB, MRFF is contacted by seventeen clients currently serving as active duty USAF noncommissioned officers who intended to reenlist in the USAF within the next nine months. These NCOs had been told specifically by their commanders that they MUST end their respective enlistment oaths with the words "so help me God" or face expulsion from the USAF. MRFF President and Founder Mikey Weintstein sends a letter on September 11, 2014, to the Secretary of Defense Chuck Hagel on behalf of these seventeen clients requesting that he immediately remediate this religiously bigoted issue and prevent any valuable airmen from being wrongfully discharged from the military for failing a blatantly unconstitutional religious test.

On September 17, 2014, the Air Force News Service (AFNS) reports: "In response to concerns raised by Airmen, the Department of the Air Force requested an opinion from the DoD General Counsel addressing the legal parameters of the oath. The resulting opinion concluded that an individual may strike or omit the words 'So help me God' from an enlistment or appointment oath if preferred."

On September 19, 2014, former presidential candidate, long-time televangelist, and 700 *Club* host Pat Robertson states: "There's a left-wing radical named [Mikey] Weinstein who has got a group about people against religion, or whatever he calls it, and he has just terrorized the Armed Forces. You think you're supposed to be tough, you're supposed to defend us, and you got one little Jewish radical who is scaring the pants off of you." When asked to comment, Mr. Weinstein states: "Pat Robertson is to human dignity and sanity and integrity and character what dog shit is to what is on the menu at a fine French restaurant."

September 19, 2014
MRFF Submits Written Testimony to House Armed Services Committee

MRFF President and Founder Mikey Weinstein receives an invitation on August 26, 2014, to testify on the subject of "Religious Accommodations in the Armed Services" before a hearing of the Military Personnel Subcommittee of the House Armed Services Committee. This hearing is scheduled to take place on Friday, September 19th at 8:00 a.m. in 2118 Rayburn House Office Building and last two hours with nongovernmental witnesses. Mikey and MRFF submit seventy-eight pages of written testimony for this hearing on September 13, 2014.

Soon after arriving in Washington, DC on September 17, 2014, in advance of the scheduled congressional hearing, it is announced that the U.S. Air Force had instructed force support offices across the service to allow both enlisted members and officers to omit the words "So help me God" from enlistment and officer appointment oaths if an Airman chooses. This is a significant victory on behalf of MRFF clients after Mikey had written to Secretary of Defense Chuck Hagel regarding this issue back in September 11, 2014 (with copies of the letters going to both the Secretary and the Chief of Staff of the U.S. Air Force).

Mikey receives an email from an MRFF client on September 18, 2014, that states:

"I was in a car repair shop waiting room on 18 September at approximately 9:00 am (Eastern) and the TV was broadcasting The 700 Club. One of the reports described the recent case in which the Air Force removed the requirement for Airmen to swear an oath to God in order to reenlist. Then the reporter was followed up by Pat Robertson with his comments."

People for the American Way (PFAW) later report on Pat Robertson's comments and provide the following transcription of those comments:

"There is a left-wing radical named Mickey Weinstein who has gotten a group about 'people against religion' or whatever he calls it and he has just terrorized the Armed Forces. You think you're supposed to be tough, you're supposed to defend us, and you've got one little Jewish radical who is scaring the pants off of you. You want these guys flying airplanes to defend us when you've got one little guy terrorizing them? That's what it amounts to. We swear oaths, 'So help me God,' what does it mean? It means, 'With God's help.' You don't have to say you believe in God, you just have to say you want some help beside myself with the oath I'm taking. It's just crazy. What is wrong with the Air Force? How can they fly the bombers to defend us if they cave to one little guy?"

Later on September 18, 2014 (the day before the scheduled congressional testimony), Mikey receives the following email from the Armed Services Committee:

Due to a late change in the legislative calendar today we are forced cancel the hearing for tomorrow. My sincerest apologies for this late change.

I would like to thank each of you for your willingness to travel to Washington to testify and for your cooperation in helping to put together this panel. We are currently working a rescheduled date and I will of course let you know as soon as we are able to settle on a future hearing date.

Once again, thanks for your time and I am sorry for this late schedule change.

No announcement of a rescheduled hearing by the Armed Services Committee has been announced as of September 24, 2014.

September 26, 2014
MRFF Speaks at Patrick Henry College

Patrick Henry College is an evangelical fundamentalist Christian college located in Purcellville, VA (about 1 hour west of Washington, D.C.) that "...seeks to recreate the original American collegiate ideal with fearless learning for Christ and His Truth. We train young leaders in the American and classical traditions with our core curriculum while centering all truth on the person and work of Jesus Christ." PHC also declares, among other things, that "... all who die outside of Christ shall be confined in conscious torment for eternity."

MRFF President/Founder Mikey Weinstein and Advisory Board Member Lawrence Wilkerson spoke at the 'Newsmakers Interview Series with Marvin Olasky' at Patrick Henry College (PHC) on September 26, 2014. This event was effectively described by two attendees who provided MRFF with the following email commentaries:

1) "Speaking on behalf of many of us who attended, I wanted to thank you for the personal courage it must have taken for you to come here. We all saw your security guards and after going to your website at the MRFF we now know why you need them. While a lot of us can't say much for Mr. Olasky's offensive, sketchy interview "techniques", we really can praise your excellent answers and instructive and even humorous commentary. You kept your cool and we learned so much. We also very much appreciated your MRFF friend Mr. Larry Wilkinson's words as well. Of my (number of years withheld) years at this school this day was the most educational day ever! And I'm not the only one who feels that way. We see things differently now and we haven't sacrificed our faith in Christ

to do that. Please know that many of us here at PHC are in your corner from now on."

2) "I'm a 20XX graduate of Patrick Henry College. Needless to say, I was pretty surprised to hear that Mikey Weinstein of MRFF was speaking there. Separation of church and state was consistently denigrated during my time there—a frightening prospect, considering that I was a government major. The campus administration seemed a bit hesitant about Mr. Weinstein's appearance as well. A few hours before his interview began, the administration sent out a campus-wide email calling Mr. Weinstein a "rather non-traditional guest" who would "bring[] an alternate and, by some standards, anti-Christian viewpoint." To their credit, the email asked the students to be hospitable. It's unfortunate, however, that separation of church and state in the military would be a topic that requires such an introduction. Marvin Olasky, of World Magazine fame, conducted the interview. From the beginning, his questioning was unnecessarily belligerent. He presumed that Mr. Weinstein's answers could be a simple yes or no (as if the law is that simple) and gave Mr. Weinstein little time to provide a detailed explanation about the various factors that would go into the legal analysis of a case. Despite Olasky's shortcom-

ings, it was a great interview. Mr. Weinstein gave as good (probably better) than he got, and the students heard a great explanation about the importance of the Establishment Clause in the military. I very much appreciated Mr. Weinstein's entering the lion's den that is my alma mater in order to provide the students with another point of view. PHC rarely, if ever, invites a guest who is not a member of the Religious Right. Its students are intentionally trained to 'bring Christ into the public square.' Giving the students a glimpse of the other side of the story is crucial."

EPILOGUE

As I have previously stated, we seriously answer every letter that comes into the Foundation in a timely fashion. Since we receive thousands upon thousands of emails, one might ask how we could possibly do that. Well, that is a very good question. We are very fortunate to have a wonderful staff of volunteers. They are an incredible group of people dedicated to the Foundation, many of whom have been with us for many years.

You have just read my presentation of a small sample of the hate letters we've received that are very poorly written and hopelessly misspelled. It continually amazes me that these people have money for computers but not for a grammar/style book!

I did not, however, include our answers and/or responses to these letters. We recently received one of those exceptionally heinous letters which fits perfectly into this book. One of our volunteers answered this particular letter, and it's one of the most succinct and perfect responses I have ever read. It is also amazingly timely! The following letter is from Jane, an Air Force wife and proud mother of soon-to-be-six children.

From: janeeslimmz@boiseebuuty.com
Subject: Take 'So Help Me God' Out of AF Oath?
Date: September 7, 2014 at 11:04:16 PM CDT
To: Mikey Weinstein <mikey@militaryreligious-freedom.org>

Really Mickey Shitface Whinesteen? Take Christ out of our Air Force oath? Hows' about we pray to Jesus to take YOU AND YOUR DISEASSED FAMILY AND THE MFRR out of America and out of this earthly life first? The flesh and bones of you and your ugly wife and retard fucktoid children will burn neverending in hells' fire. Along with your fellow jew plotters of Joan River and Robin William. What, dont hear anyone laughing now huh Mickey? They got theres and you get yours. We pray your next. You think you can beat Jesus out of the Air Force? Jesus will beat your jew ass like a fucking drum. HalleJEWyuh! HATE YOU. Jane. I am wife of AF lifer and mom of 5 and 1 on the way)

This is what our volunteer wrote back to this wonderful mother:

Subject: Re: Take 'So Help Me God' Out of AF
Oath?
Date: September 8, 2014
To: janeeslimmz@boiseebuuty.com

Good morning Jane,

I'm just going to leave a few things here for you to
consider:

Colossians 3:8 ESV / 38 helpful votes

But now you must put them all away: anger,
wrath, malice, slander, and obscene talk from your
mouth.

Ephesians 4:31 ESV / 34 helpful votes

Let all bitterness and wrath and anger and clamor
and slander be put away from you, along with all
malice.

James 1:26 ESV / 33 helpful votes

If anyone thinks he is religious and does not bridle
his tongue but deceives his heart, this person's religion is worthless.

You really must hate your god to disobey him so vehemently. But hey, if you want to re-invent Christianity and recast your precious Jesus as a hate-filled monstrosity, by all means, carry on. Ignorance like that will do nothing but marginalize your religion to a point of irrelevance in short order.

P.S.: Jesus was never in the oath. Can't remove something that wasn't there to begin with

That being said, I really don't see an end to the hate here if wonderful mothers like this one continue to teach and preach such crapola to their children. They feel free to throw out this kind of hate to everyone they perceive to be "evil" or to anyone who happens to have a differing opinion. It is patently sad when I stop to think that she kisses her children with that foul mouth!